# Close-Up
English in Use
TEACHER'S BOOK

B1

Philip James

Australia • Brazil • Japan • Korea • Mexico • Singapore • Spain • United Kingdom • United States

Contents

Unit	Grammar	Vocabulary
1 pages 4–9	present simple; adverbs of frequency; present continuous; stative verbs	collocations & expressions; sentence transformation; word formation; speaking
2 pages 10-14	countable nouns; uncountable nouns; quantifiers	prepositions; open cloze; sentence transformation; writing
3 pages 15-19	past simple; past continuous	phrasal verbs; sentence transformation; word formation; speaking
4 pages 20-24	*used to* & *would*; *be used to* & *get used to*	word formation; open cloze; cloze; writing
Review 1 pages 25-28	Grammar Use of English: sentence transformation; word formation; Grammar & Vocabulary	
5 pages 29-34	present perfect simple; *have been* & *have gone*; *ago, for* & *since*; present perfect simple & past simple; present perfect continuous; present perfect simple & present perfect continuous	prepositions; cloze; word formation; speaking
6 pages 35-39	the indefinite article: *a/an*; the definite article: *the*	collocations & expressions; open cloze; sentence transformation; writing
7 pages 40-44	relative clauses; defining relative clauses; non-defining relative clauses	word formation; sentence transformation; open cloze; speaking
8 pages 45-48	temporals	phrasal verbs; word formation; open cloze; writing
Review 2 pages 49-52	Grammar Use of English: open cloze; word formation; Grammar & Vocabulary	
9 pages 53-58	future simple; *be going to*	prepositions; open cloze; cloze; speaking
10 pages 59-64	future continuous; future perfect simple	collocations & expressions; open cloze; cloze; writing
11 pages 65-70	zero conditional; first conditional; second conditional; *unless*	phrasal verbs; cloze; sentence transformation; speaking
12 pages 71-75	third conditional; *wish* & *if only*	word formation; open cloze; word formation; writing
Review 3 pages 76-80	Grammar Use of English: word formation; sentence transformation; Grammar & Vocabulary	

Unit	Grammar	Vocabulary
13 pages 81-85	past perfect simple; past simple & past perfect simple; past perfect continuous	prepositions; open cloze; cloze; speaking
14 pages 86-91	question tags; subject and object questions; negative questions	collocations & expressions; sentence transformation; cloze; writing
15 pages 92-97	can & could; may & might; must; should; would; needn't; be able to; have to; mustn't & don't have to	word formation; cloze; sentence transformation; speaking
16 pages 98-102	may/might have; should have; could have; can't/couldn't have; must have; would have	phrasal verbs; open cloze; word formation; writing
Review 4 pages 103-106	Grammar Use of English: word formation; open cloze; Grammar & Vocabulary	
17 pages 107-111	the passive voice: tenses; by & with	prepositions; open cloze; cloze; speaking
18 pages 112-115	the passive voice: gerunds, infinitives & modal	phrasal verbs; open cloze; cloze; speaking
19 pages 116-121	reported speech: statements; say & tell; reported speech: changes in time & place	word formation; exam practice; writing
20 pages 122-127	eported speech: questions; reported speech: commands; reported speech: requests; reported speech: reporting verbs	word formation; word formation; sentence transformation; writing
Review 5 pages 127-131	Grammar Use of English: word formation; open cloze; Grammar & Vocabulary	
21 pages 132-136	causative	collocations & expressions; cloze; sentence transformation; speaking
22 pages 137-141	gerunds; infinitives; full infinitives; bare infinitives; gerund or infinitive?	prepositions; open cloze; word formation; writing
23 pages 142-146	order of adjectives; adjectives ending in -ed & -ing; types of adverbs; order of adverbs (manner, place & time); order of adverbs (degree & frequency); so & such	phrasal verbs; word formation; cloze; speaking
24 pages 147-151	comparison of adjectives & adverbs; other comparative structures	word formation; cloze; sentence transformation; writing
Review 6 pages 152-155	Grammar Use of English: open cloze; word formation; Grammar & Vocabulary	

Irregular Verbs	156	Collocations & Expressions	161
Phrasal verbs	158	Word formation	162
Prepositions	160		

Unit 1

Awareness

1 Which of these sentences are correct (C) and incorrect (I)?

1 Mum's plane arrives at 10.15. _C_
2 My grandfather is always saying I'm lazy. _C_
3 Oh no! It snows very heavily at the moment. _I_
4 She's thinking about going home for the holidays. _C_
5 You're seeming angry. Did I do something? _I_
6 Are you believing there is life on Mars? _I_
7 Kevin likes visiting his cousins in Wales. _C_
8 My parents live in the city centre. _C_
9 I'm not understanding why you fight with your little brother. _I_
10 What do you think about right now? _I_

How many did you get right? ☐

Grammar
Present Simple

Affirmative	Negative	Questions
I/we/you/they walk he/she/it walk**s**	I/we/you/they **don't** walk he/she/it **doesn't** walk	**Do** I/we/you/they walk? **Does** he/she/it walk?
Short Answers		
Yes, I/we/you/they **do**. **Yes**, he/she/it **does**.	**No**, I/we/you/they **don't**. **No**, he/she/it **doesn't**.	

We use the Present Simple for
• facts or general truths.
*The sun **rises** in the east.*
• routines or habits (often with adverbs of frequency).
*He often **watches** TV in the evenings.*
• permanent states.
*She **works** in the city centre.*
• timetabled events in the future.
*My English lesson **starts** at two o'clock this afternoon.*

Note

Some common time expressions that are often used with the Present Simple are *every day/week/month/summer, every other day, once a week, twice a month, at the weekend, in January, in the morning/afternoon/evening, at night, on Tuesdays, on Friday mornings,* etc.
*I walk my dog **every morning**.*

Adverbs of Frequency

We use adverbs of frequency to say how often something happens. They come before the main verb, but after the verb *be*.
*Sheila **is always** busy at the weekends.*
*Jason **hardly ever eats** out at restaurants.*
*Dad **never shouts** at me or my brother.*

Some common adverbs of frequency are:
always ↓ (most often)   sometimes
usually   rarely / hardly ever / seldom
often   never ↓ (least often)

Present Continuous

Affirmative	Negative	Questions
I **am** ('**m**) walk**ing** he/she/it **is** ('**s**) walk**ing** we/you/they **are** ('**re**) walk**ing**	I **am** ('**m**) **not** walk**ing** he/she/it **is not** (**isn't**) walk**ing** we/you/they **are not** (**aren't**) walk**ing**	**Am** I walk**ing**? **Is** he/she/it walk**ing**? **Are** we/you/they walk**ing**?
Short Answers		
Yes, I **am**. **Yes**, he/she/it **is**. **Yes**, we/you/they **are**.	**No**, I'm **not**. **No**, he/she/it **isn't**. **No**, we/you/they **aren't**.	

Spelling: ta**k**e → ta**k**ing, ge**t** → ge**tt**ing, fl**y** → fl**y**ing

We use the Present Continuous for
- actions that are in progress at or around the time of speaking.
We're making a birthday cake for Mum right now.
- actions that are temporary.
I'm looking after my sister's dog this week.
- situations that are changing or developing in the present.
More and more families *are having* financial problems.
- an annoying habit (often with *always, continually, constantly* and *forever*).
My mother *is continually telling* me to tidy up my room.
- plans and arrangements for the future.
We're having a family get-together on Saturday evening.

> **Note**
> Some common time expressions that are often used with the Present Continuous are *at the moment, now, for the time being, this morning/afternoon/evening/week/month/year, today,* etc.
> My younger brother is staying with me **for the time being**.

Stative Verbs

Some verbs are not usually used in continuous tenses. They are called stative because they describe states and not actions. To talk about the present, we use these verbs in the Present Simple tense. The most common of these are:
- verbs of emotion: *hate, like, love, need, prefer, want*
Peter **hates** his new school.
- verbs of senses: *feel, hear, see, smell, sound, taste*
These flowers **smell** wonderful.
- verbs which express a state of mind: *believe, doubt, forget, imagine, know, remember, seem, suppose, think, understand*
I **doubt** Dad will be home in time for dinner.
- verbs of possession: *belong to, have, own, possess*
Do you know who **owns** that car parked in the street?
- other verbs: *be, consist, contain, cost, include, mean*
The price **includes** flights and accommodation.

Some verbs can be both stative verbs and action verbs, but with a different meaning. The most common of these verbs are:

be	Pat **is** very reliable. (usual behaviour) Tony **is being** naughty. (at the moment; not his normal behaviour)
expect	I **expect** Mum will go to the shops on her way home. (expect = think or believe) We'**re expecting** an email from my older sister. (expect = wait for)
have	Penny **has** a huge garden. (have = own/possess) Trent **is having** a great time at his grandparents' house. (have = experience) Brad **is having** lunch with his aunt and uncle today. (have = eating)
look	He **looks** like his father. (look like = resemble) **Are you looking** for your blue jacket? (look = search)
taste	This sauce **tastes** awful! (taste = have a particular flavour) Why **are you tasting** the soup? (taste = test the flavour)
think	I **think** Uncle Ben is very funny. (think = have an opinion) Janet'**s thinking** of visiting her parents this weekend. (think = consider)
see	'My aunt Sue is my dad's sister.' 'Oh, I **see**.' (see = understand) 'I'**m seeing** my cousin later today.' (see = meet)
smell	This soap **smells** like roses. (smell = have a particular smell) Why **are you smelling** the meat? (smell = action of smelling)
weigh	Pete **weighs** 53 kg. (weigh = have a particular weight) I'**m weighing** myself to see how heavy I am. (weigh = measure the weight)

Unit 1

Grammar Exercises

2 Choose the correct answers.

1 Stop that, William! Why ___ so naughty this morning?
   a are you be
   b are you being

2 Who's that? I ___ her name.
   a 'm not remembering
   b don't remember

3 Irene ___ with her cousin for the time being.
   a lives
   b is living

4 Grandpa isn't feeling well. He ___ the doctor later today.
   a 's seeing
   b sees

5 Penny ___ of getting her children a pet.
   a is thinking
   b thinks

6 Tony ___ his grandfather.
   a is looking like
   b looks like

7 Mum and Dad always ___ us with them on holidays.
   a take
   b are taking

8 Grandma ___ the sauce at the moment to see if it's too salty.
   a tastes
   b is tasting

9 Bob and Sue ___ to their aunt Maisie's house every weekend.
   a are going
   b go

10 Why ___ so many families can't get along?
   a do you think
   b are you thinking

3 Complete the sentences with the correct form of the Present Simple or Present Continuous of the verbs in brackets.

1 Sherry _____'s finding_____ (find) it hard to make new friends. She _____doesn't seem_____ (not seem) to be able to meet people easily.

2 Look! It _____'s raining_____ (rain). It _____rarely rains_____ (rarely / rain) in Greece in the summer.

3 Joey _____is seeing_____ (see) a dentist about his toothache tomorrow.

4 She _____'s riding_____ (ride) her bike at the moment. She _____rides_____ (ride) her bike every evening before she _____has_____ (have) dinner.

5 Mum _____gets_____ (get) a call from my brother, Steve, twice a week. He _____'s travelling_____ (travel) around Europe and _____never forgets_____ (never / forget) to phone her.

6 When I _____do_____ (do) something nice for my family, I _____feel_____ (feel) great!

7 Tony can't come out to play because he _____'s doing_____ (do) his homework. He _____does_____ (do) his homework every afternoon at this time.

8 _____Do they always phone_____ (they / always / phone) your grandparents before they go to visit?

4 Match the questions to the answers.

1. Do your grandparents live in the countryside? — *h*
2. Where are you and your family going on holiday this summer? — *j*
3. Do I have ice cream on my nose? — *c*
4. Is it cold out today? — *e*
5. Are the children doing their homework? — *g*
6. What is the dog eating now? — *a*
7. Is your uncle a mechanic? — *d*
8. Does your aunt work at the post office? — *i*
9. How often do you go to the gym? — *f*
10. Are you going to the cinema with your parents tonight? — *b*

a A bone.
b No, I'm not.
c Yes, you do.
d No, he isn't.
e Yes, it is.
f Every week.
g Yes, they are.
h No, they don't.
i Yes, she does.
j Canada.

5 Complete the sentences with the correct form of the Present Simple and Present Continuous of the verbs in bold.

1. **be**
   a My sister _____is_____ a polite, honest, reasonable person.
   b Why ___are you being___ (you) so mean to your baby brother today?
2. **see**
   a He ___'s seeing___ the family doctor later this week.
   b Do you ___see___ what I mean now?
3. **weigh**
   a How much ___does your father weigh___ (your father)?
   b The butcher ___is weighing___ the meat now to see if it's more than what I asked for.
4. **expect**
   a I ___expect___ my mother will be angry with me for not tidying the house.
   b She ___'s expecting___ a package from her daughter in the post today.
5. **have**
   a Your grandparents ___have___ a really nice home.
   b What time ___are you having___ (you) lunch with Tom today?
6. **look**
   a You really ___look___ like your sister. Are you twins?
   b What ___are you looking___ (you) for now? You're always losing things.

6 Use the prompts to write questions. Use the correct form of the verbs.

1. you / eat / with your parents / every evening?
   Do you eat with your parents every evening?
2. what time / your dad / usually / get home from work?
   What time does your dad usually get home from work?
3. how many languages / your cousin / speak?
   How many languages does your cousin speak?
4. you / wash / your hair at the moment?
   Are you washing your hair at the moment?
5. why / your little sister / laugh?
   Why is your little sister laughing?
6. who / you / usually / walk / to school with?
   Who do you usually walk to school with?
7. she / think / of moving back home with her parents?
   Is she thinking of moving back home with her parents?
8. why / you / smell / the meat?
   Why are you smelling the meat?

Unit 1

7 Write questions to the answers.

1 **A:** What _does he usually do on Saturdays_ ?
  B: He usually visits relatives on Saturdays.
2 **A:** What time _does she make lunch every day_ ?
  B: She makes lunch at twelve o'clock every day.
3 **A:** Where _does your brother live_ ?
  B: My brother lives in Glasgow.
4 **A:** What _are you doing this weekend_ ?
  B: I'm going to a family picnic this weekend.
5 **A:** When _does the school dance take place_ ?
  B: The school dance takes place on Friday night.
6 **A:** Why _are you smelling the soap_ ?
  B: I'm smelling the soap to see if it smells nice.
7 **A:** How often _do you walk the dog_ ?
  B: I walk the dog twice a day.
8 **A:** Whose _car are you washing at the moment_ ?
  B: I'm washing Dad's car at the moment; then I'll do Mum's.

Vocabulary

Collocations & Expressions

8 Complete the phrases using these verbs. You will need to use each verb twice.

fall   get   have   keep   pay

1 _pay_ a compliment
2 _keep_ a diary
3 _have_ a family
4 _keep_ a secret
5 _pay_ a visit
6 _get_ divorced
7 _fall_ in love
8 _get_ married
9 _have_ sympathy
10 _fall_ to pieces

9 Complete the sentences with the correct form of the expressions from 8.

1 After 20 years, Susie's parents are _getting divorced_; naturally she's very upset.
2 Sam's father left his mother. Sam's worried that she'll _fall to pieces_.
3 I _have_ a lot of _sympathy_ for children of separated or divorced parents.
4 My grandmother's house is near here; let's go _pay_ her _a visit_.
5 Mum, do you remember what it was that made you _fall in love_ with Dad?
6 Pam, can you _keep a secret_? Good, come here and I'll whisper it in your ear.
7 A lot of my friends _keep a diary_; they write in it every day.
8 My sister is _getting married_ at the end of the month – she's having a traditional white wedding.
9 'Do you plan to _have a family_ when you grow up?' 'I want a big one with five children!'
10 My boyfriend _paid_ me _a compliment_ today; he said I was very pretty!

Exam Practice

Sentence transformation

10 Complete the second sentence so that it has a similar meaning to the first sentence, using the word given. Do not change the word given. You must use between two and five words.

1 I have an appointment to see the dentist on Monday.
   am
   I _____ *am seeing* _____ the dentist on Monday.

2 They seldom go anywhere without their children.
   often
   They _____ *don't often go* _____ anywhere without their children.

3 Susie goes to the pool every Monday and Wednesday with her mum.
   twice
   Susie goes to the pool _____ *twice a week* _____ with her mum.

4 Tim resembles Tammy because they are twins.
   like
   Tim _____ *looks like* _____ Tammy because they are twins.

5 My mother complains about my messy bedroom all the time.
   continually
   My mother _____ *is continually complaining* _____ about my messy bedroom.

6 Fran nearly always does her homework before she has dinner.
   hardly
   Fran _____ *hardly ever does her homework* _____ after dinner.

7 My baby brother is very light!
   weigh
   My baby brother _____ *doesn't weigh* _____ much!

8 The temperature is dropping every day; winter is coming.
   getting
   It _____ *'s getting colder* _____ every day; winter is coming.

Word formation

11 Use the word in capitals to form a word that fits in the gap.

1 _____ *Genetics* _____ is a science that helps you find out about your family history. **GENE**
2 How many of your _____ *relatives* _____ were at the family get-together last week? **RELATE**
3 I think _____ *marriage* _____ is important if you want to start a family. **MARRY**
4 Tom is always on time; he's very _____ *reliable* _____. **RELY**
5 My dad is a(n) _____ *reasonable* _____ man, so I often go to him for advice. **REASON**
6 My grandmother is a(n) _____ *elderly* _____ woman with glasses and grey hair. **ELDER**
7 I can't see why your brother is so _____ *arrogant* _____; there's nothing special about him! **ARROGANCE**
8 Elephants show signs that they _____ *grieve* _____ when one of their family member dies. **GRIEF**

What Do You Think?

Speaking

 **Discuss these questions with a partner:**

- How many people are there in your family?
- How many brothers/sisters/cousins have you got?
- Do you think it's better to have a big or small family? Why?
- How often do you go on holiday with your family?
- Are you doing anything fun with your parents this weekend? What?

Unit 2

Awareness

1 Which of these sentences are correct (C) and incorrect (I)?

1 Did Sam do any homework at the weekend? C
2 There isn't much food in the house. C
3 My parents works for the same company. I
4 Maths is very difficult for some students. C
5 Is there some rubbish in the bin? I
6 I've got three cousin – Tony, Joe and Sue. I
7 Can I borrow some money from you, please? C
8 Are there some tomatoes in the fridge? I
9 Salt aren't good for your health. I
10 There is a bowl of fruit on the table. C

How many did you get right? ☐

Grammar

Countable Nouns

Most nouns are countable and have singular and plural forms.

sister – sisters   family – families   toy – toys   tomato – tomatoes
leaf – leaves   child – children   woman – women   foot – feet

We usually use *a* or *an* with singular countable nouns.
a family get-together
an idea

We can use *some*, *any* or a number (e.g. *two*) with plural countable nouns.
There are **some** cats in the garden.
Are there **any** oranges?
My sister's wedding is in **two** weeks.

We use singular or plural verb forms with countable nouns depending on whether we are talking about one or more items.
A family holiday **is** just what they need.
My brothers live in Leeds.

> **Note**
>
> Some countable nouns don't end in *-s*. Remember to use a plural verb form with them.
>
> **Children are** usually friendly.
> The **women are** in the garden.

Uncountable Nouns

Some nouns are uncountable. They do not have plural forms.

advice   food   history   luggage   progress   time
cheese   fruit   homework   milk   research   traffic
chocolate   fun   information   money   rubbish   water
equipment   furniture   knowledge   music   salt   weather

We don't use *a* or *an* with uncountable nouns. We can use *some* and *any*.
I'd like **some** salt in my soup.
Have they got **any** information about your missing dog?

We always use singular verb forms with uncountable nouns.
This chocolate **is** so delicious.
Fruit **is** good for you.

We can use phrases describing quantity with uncountable nouns to say how much we have.
The most common of these phrases are:

- a bag of
- a bottle of
- a bowl of
- a can of
- a carton of
- a cup of
- a glass of
- a jar of
- a kilo of
- a loaf of
- a number of
- a packet of
- a piece of
- a tin of

I'll prepare **a bowl of** fruit.
Would you like **a glass of** juice?

> **Note**
>
> Some uncountable nouns end in *-s*. Remember to use a singular verb form with them.
>
> The **news is** very good!
> **Physics isn't** an easy subject.

10

Quantifiers

We use *some* with both uncountable and plural countable nouns in affirmative sentences and in requests or offers.
Here are **some magazines** for you to read.
Can you send me **some information**, please?
Would you like **some cheese** on your sandwich?

We use *any* with both uncountable and plural countable nouns in negative sentences and in questions.
Billy hasn't got **any sisters**.
Did Mum buy **any chocolate** at the shops?

We use *a lot / lots of* with both uncountable and plural countable nouns.
I've got **lots of luggage** to take on my trip.
There are **a lot of people** in this city.

We use *a little* with uncountable nouns and *a few* with plural countable nouns in affirmative sentences.
I like **a little sugar** in my coffee.
Kevin always has **a few sandwiches** for lunch.

We use *much* with uncountable nouns and *many* with plural countable nouns in negative sentences and in questions.
There wasn't **much rain** last year.
Have you got **many friends**, Steve?

Grammar Exercises

2 Write countable (C) or uncountable (U).

1 brother   *C*
2 woman   *C*
3 traffic   *U*
4 weather   *U*
5 tomato   *C*
6 family   *C*
7 equipment *U*
8 foot   *C*
9 furniture *U*
10 research   *U*
11 toy   *C*
12 news   *U*
13 knowledge *U*
14 maths   *U*
15 child   *C*

3 Complete the dialogues with *a*, *an* or *some*.

1 **A:** Can I have ____*an*____ orange, please?
   B: Of course!
2 **A:** What's that, Dad?
   B: It's ____*an*____ old watch that Grandpa gave me.
3 **A:** I saw ____*some*____ cool computer equipment and ____*an*____ amazing MP3 player in a shop this morning.
   B: Oh, did you buy anything?
4 **A:** Mum wants to make ____*an*____ apple pie, but there are only two apples.
   B: Oh, well, I'll go and buy ____*some*____.
5 **A:** What did you get for your birthday?
   B: I got ____*some*____ delicious chocolate and ____*a*____ great book!
6 **A:** Could I have ____*some*____ milk?
   B: Oh, there isn't any left.
7 **A:** Did you buy ____*a*____ gift for your grandmother?
   B: Yes, I bought her ____*an*____ Italian silk scarf.
8 **A:** Do you want ____*some*____ sugar in your tea?
   B: No, thanks. It's fine.
9 **A:** I'm going to the shops. Should I get ____*a*____ loaf of bread?
   B: Yes, please, and ____*a*____ carton of juice.
10 **A:** Would you like ____*some*____ fruit, Maria?
   B: Yes, I'd like ____*a*____ peach.

Unit 2

4 Circle the correct words.

1 How many children was / **were** there at your sister's party?
2 Some people never eats / **eat** fruit.
3 There **is** / are a carton of milk in the fridge.
4 Maths **is** / are Jody's favourite subject at school.
5 I can't find the baby's toys. Where is / **are** they?
6 The music **is** / are too loud! Turn it down.
7 Dad's feet is / **are** huge!
8 The advice you gave me **was** / were very helpful.
9 I'm afraid the news about your son **isn't** / aren't good.
10 My parents is / **are** visiting friends at the moment.

5 Complete the dialogue with some or any.

Mum: There isn't (1) ___any___ food in this house! We'd better go to the supermarket, Julie.

Julie: OK, Mum, I'll make a list. Tell me what we need.

Mum: Let's see. Well, we need (2) ___some___ bread and pasta. We haven't got (3) ___any___ eggs or flour either.

Julie: Oh, are there (4) ___any___ tins of tomato sauce left?

Mum: No, so we need (5) ___some___ of those. And we need (6) ___some___ fresh fruit and frozen vegetables.

Julie: Right. Is there (7) ___any___ cheese in the fridge?

Mum: Yes, there is (8) ___some___ cheese, but there isn't (9) ___any___ butter or (10) ___any___ cartons of milk.

Julie: Alright! That must be it. Let's go. I hope you've got (11) ___some___ money, Mum, because I haven't got (12) ___any___!

6 Choose the correct answers.

1 Here are ___ biscuits for you, Marge.
  a a little
  b much
  c some

2 Can you give me ___ advice, Dad?
  a some
  b any
  c a few

3 Would you like ___ tea, Aunt Edna?
  a lot of
  b some
  c many

4 Did your sister have ___ music at her wedding?
  a lots
  b a few
  c any

5 Many young people haven't got ___ knowledge of old family traditions.
  a any
  b many
  c some

6 I've got ___ time to play with my cousins today!
  a a few
  b much
  c lots of

7 There are ___ children in the park today.
  a a lot of
  b a little
  c lots

8 Grandma likes ___ sugar and milk in her hot chocolate.
  a a few
  b a little
  c many

9 Let's take a look at ___ wedding traditions from around the world.
  a a few
  b much
  c a lot

10 How ___ of you keep a diary?
  a much
  b some
  c many

7 Find the mistakes and correct the sentences where necessary. Put a tick (✓) below those which do not need correcting.

1. There were a large number of people at my brother's wedding.
   There was a large number of people at my brother's wedding.
2. In Japan, the womans getting married wear white kimonos.
   In Japan, the women getting married wear white kimonos.
3. Children is usually upset when their parents get divorced.
   Children are usually upset when their parents get divorced.
4. My family history is very interesting.
   ✓
5. Do you know what the weather is supposed to be like tomorrow?
   ✓
6. Were there a lot of traffic when you were on your way to work?
   Was there a lot of traffic when you were on your way to work?
7. Sarah, can you buy a loaf of milk on your way home?
   Sarah, can you buy a carton of milk / a loaf of bread on your way home?
8. My sister always gets paid lots of compliments on her looks.
   ✓

Vocabulary

Prepositions

8 Circle the correct prepositions.

1. friends **of** / from mine
2. throw a little **over** / in your shoulder
3. walked slowly at / **through**
4. decorates it **with** / for pretty ribbons
5. covered **from** / around head to toe
6. pin money at / **to**
7. at the end **of** / on
8. with / **for** good luck
9. with / **in** countries
10. take a look over / **at**

9 Complete the sentences with the correct form of the prepositional phrases from 8.

1. Traditions vary greatly ____*in countries*____ around the world.
2. ____*Take a look at*____ the bride! She's beautiful!
3. Some ____*friends of mine*____ have got divorced parents.
4. The bride plants a tree and ____*decorates it with pretty ribbons*____.
5. In many countries, guests ____*pin money to*____ the bride's dress.
6. ____*At the end of*____ my aunt's wedding ceremony we threw rice at her and her new husband.
7. The bride was ____*covered from head to toe*____ in paint!
8. Brides need to have 'something old, something new, something borrowed and something blue' ____*for good luck*____.
9. There is a tradition that when you spill salt, you ____*throw a little over your shoulder*____.
10. As part of the ceremony, the couple ____*walked slowly through*____ the town.

Unit 2

Exam Practice

Open cloze

10 Complete the sentences with the word that best fits each gap.

1. Were there _____*many*_____ people at your grandfather's 90 birthday?
2. I don't want to fall _____*in*_____ love until I'm middle-aged!
3. The guests threw sweets and nuts _____*at*_____ the happy couple.
4. When you _____*get*_____ married, will you wear a white dress?
5. We decorated the house _____*with*_____ lots of pretty flowers and ribbons.
6. I _____*have*_____ a lot of sympathy for children whose parents are divorced.
7. Friends _____*of*_____ my husband are coming to visit this evening.
8. There were _____*lots*_____ of people at the party after the wedding.

Sentence transformation

11 Complete the second sentence so that it has a similar meaning to the first sentence, using the word given. Do not change the word given. You must use between two and five words.

1. This sauce is really salty!
   too
   There _____*is too much salt*_____ in this sauce!

2. Shall I put sugar in your coffee?
   some
   Would you _____*like some sugar*_____ in your coffee?

3. Can you tell me the number of people who are coming to the wedding?
   how
   Can you tell me _____*how many people*_____ are coming to the wedding?

4. Dan and Helen are having their wedding on Saturday.
   getting
   Dan and Helen are _____*getting married*_____ on Saturday.

5. Mum hasn't got much spare time to cook today.
   a
   Mum's only got _____*a little time*_____ to cook today.

6. There are only two biscuits left in the bag.
   many
   There _____*aren't many*_____ biscuits left in the bag.

7. She said nice things about my wedding dress.
   compliment
   She _____*paid me a compliment*_____ on my wedding dress.

8. I wonder if this café serves different kinds of meat dishes.
   any
   I wonder if there _____*are any meat dishes*_____ on the menu in this café.

What Do You Think?

Writing

12 Read the writing task below and write the email in your notebook. Try to use linking words like *also*, *as well*, *and*, *too*, *as*, *since*, *because*, *such as* and *for example*.

Your grandparents have been married for 50 years and your family is having a family get-together to celebrate. Write an email to one of your relatives inviting him/her to the party.

Awareness

1 Which of these sentences are correct (C) and incorrect (I)?

1. Paul was eating all the biscuits this morning.   I
2. Sue was making a cake at two o'clock yesterday afternoon.   C
3. They wasn't having a snack when I arrived.   I
4. Tom never ate meat when he was younger.   C
5. We weren't going out to eat last week.   I
6. The rain was falling and the children were looking sadly out the window.   C
7. Ken and I tidyed the kitchen earlier today.   I
8. Did your aunt made an apple pie yesterday?   I
9. Dad peeled the potatoes and fried them an hour ago.   C
10. Were they eating their lunch when somebody knocked at the door?   C

How many did you get right? ☐

Grammar
Past Simple

Affirmative	Negative	Questions
I/he/she/it/we/you/they chew**ed**	I/he/she/it/we/you/they **didn't** chew	**Did** I/he/she/it/we/you/they **chew**?
Short Answers		
Yes, I/he/she/it **did**. **Yes**, we/you/they **did**.	**No**, we/you/they **didn't**. **No**, I/he/she/it **didn't**.	

Spelling: dance → danc**ed**, travel → trave**lled**, tidy → ti**died**, play → play**ed**

We use the Past Simple for
- something that started and finished in the past.
*Mum **made** some sandwiches an hour ago.*
- past routines and habits (often with adverbs of frequency).
*Petra always **ate** her lunch in the school canteen.*
- actions that happened one after the other in the past, for example when telling a story.
*The family **went** home and **had** a tasty dinner.*

> **Note**
> Some verbs are irregular and do not follow these spelling rules. See a list of irregular verbs on pages 156–157.

> **Note**
> Some common time expressions that are often used with the Past Simple are *yesterday, last night/week/month/summer, a week/month/year ago, twice a week, once a month, at the weekend, in March, in the morning/afternoon/evening, at night, on Thursdays, on Monday mornings*, etc.
> *The farmer planted some olive trees **last month**.*

Past Continuous

Affirmative	Negative	Questions
I/he/she/it **was** chew**ing** we/you/they **were** chew**ing**	I/he/she/it **was not (wasn't)** chew**ing** we/you/they **were not (weren't)** chew**ing**	**Was** I/he/she/it chew**ing**? **Were** we/you/they chew**ing**?
Short Answers		
Yes, I/he/she/it **was**. **Yes**, we/you/they **were**.	**No**, I/he/she/it **wasn't**. **No**, we/you/they **weren't**.	

Spelling: dance → danc**ing**, travel → trave**lling**, tidy → tidy**ing**

Unit 3

We use the Past Continuous for
- actions that were in progress at a specific time in the past.

*Dad **was making** a pasta salad for the children at six o'clock last night.*
- two or more actions that were in progress at the same time in the past.

*I **was baking** while my sister **was doing** the washing-up.*
- giving background information in a story.

*The sun **was shining** and the birds **were singing** in the trees when suddenly they **heard** a strange sound.*
- an action that was in progress in the past that was interrupted by another.

*They **were getting** ready to have breakfast when the telephone **rang**.*

> **Note**
>
> Some common time expressions that are often used with the Past Continuous are *while, as, all day/week/month/year, at ten o'clock last night, last Sunday/week/year, this morning,* etc.
>
> *Grandma was cooking **all day**.*

Grammar Exercises

2 Circle the correct words.

1. Tony (was having) / was haveing a snack at twelve o'clock last night.
2. Were they going / (Did they go) on a picnic last weekend?
3. (Was Susie chopping) / Did Susie chopped onions a few minutes ago?
4. My grandmother usually was baking / (baked) bread twice a week.
5. Dad was frying the burgers while we (were making) / make a salad.
6. I took / (was taking) the tray out of the oven when I burnt my hand.
7. I came home, went into the kitchen and was boiling / (boiled) water for tea.
8. Pam (wasn't doing) / didn't do the washing-up when I arrived.
9. Kevin (broke) / was breaking the water jug this morning.
10. My mother weren't making / (didn't make) lunch today.

3 Complete the sentences with the correct form of the Past Simple or Past Continuous of the verbs in brackets.

1. The farmer _____*was watering*_____ (water) the tomatoes while his helper was picking some carrots.
2. Steven _____*wasn't peeling*_____ (not peel) vegetables when he cut his finger.
3. _____*Did they eat*_____ (they / eat) in a fancy restaurant last Tuesday?
4. My father always _____*took*_____ (take) his lunch to school when he was a boy.
5. _____*Were you preparing*_____ (you / prepare) breakfast when the lights went out?
6. The chef beat the eggs, _____*added*_____ (add) some salt and poured the mixture into a baking dish.
7. My sister _____*didn't fry*_____ (not fry) the eggs an hour ago; they're still hot.
8. The birds _____*were singing*_____ (sing) and the sun was shining brightly in the sky.

4 Find the mistakes and correct the sentences where necessary. Put a tick (✓) below those which do not need correcting.

1 She was making spaghetti and meatballs for dinner last night.
   She made spaghetti and meatballs for dinner last night.

2 Did they have vegetarian dishes at their dinner party?
   ✓

3 My parents weren't having time for breakfast this morning.
   My parents didn't have time for breakfast this morning.

4 Was Peter taking a cooking course all last month?
   ✓

5 I was believing her when she said she'd take me out for a meal.
   I believed her when she said she'd take me out for a meal.

6 Celia was hungry, but I was starving!
   ✓

7 My brother was making the sandwiches while I made some orange juice.
   My brother was making the sandwiches while I was making some orange juice.

8 We didn't eat our lunch when Sheila knocked on the door.
   We weren't eating our lunch when Sheila knocked on the door.

5 Complete the sentences with the word that best fits each gap.

1 The students ___were___ eating in the gym this morning – they got into trouble.
2 ___Was___ he sitting in the café when you saw him?
3 We ___did___ not have breakfast at eight o'clock this morning; we had it at nine o'clock.
4 ___Were___ you baking bread all morning?
5 My cousin was peeling potatoes ___while___ I was chopping onions.
6 I was ___not___ tidying up the kitchen at two o'clock yesterday afternoon; I was eating.
7 Mark was working in the garden ___when___ it started raining.
8 ___Did___ you go to the new French restaurant last week?

6 Find the mistake and write A or B in the box. Then write the correct sentences.

1 Janet was talking (A) on the phone when the chip pan was catching (B) fire. **B**
   Janet was talking on the phone when the chip pan caught fire.

2 Joe was surfing the Net when (A) his mother was working (B) in the kitchen. **A**
   Joe was surfing the Net while his mother was working in the kitchen.

3 Pat was opening (A) the cupboard door and took out (B) the jar of honey. **A**
   Pat opened the cupboard door and took out the jar of honey.

4 While we were (A) on holidays, we were eating (B) in restaurants every evening. **B**
   While we were on holidays we ate in restaurants every evening.

5 At eight o'clock last night, Dad was making (A) French fries while I studied (B). **B**
   At eight o' clock last night, Dad was making French fries while I was studying.

6 While Pete was planting (A) corn, Stewart watered (B) the strawberries. **B**
   While Pete was planting corn, Stewart was watering the strawberries.

Unit 3

7 Write questions using the correct form of the Past Simple or Past Continuous, then complete the short answers.

1 we / have coffee / at the local café / twice a week
   A: _Did we have at the local café twice a week_?
   B: No, _we didn't_.

2 your parents / make breakfast / while / you sleep
   A: _Were your parents making breakfast while you were sleeping_?
   B: No, _they weren't_.

3 he / take a cooking course / every winter / when / he live in France
   A: _Did he take a cooking course every winter when he lived in France_?
   B: Yes, _he did_.

4 your aunt / always / bake pies / when / she be a young woman
   A: _Did your aunt always bake pies and cakes when she was a young woman_?
   B: No, _she didn't_.

5 Sarah and Jake / clean fish / at two o'clock yesterday afternoon
   A: _Were Sarah and Jake cleaning fish at two o'clock yesterday afternoon_?
   B: Yes, _they were_.

6 Jane / on a diet / all last month
   A: _Was Jane on a diet all last month_?
   B: No, _she wasn't_.

Vocabulary

Phrasal verbs

8 Match the phrasal verbs with their meanings.

1	break off	_i_	a	to find something
2	go off	_j_	b	to go to a restaurant
3	come across	_a_	c	to reduce
4	cut down	_c_	d	to remove the skin or outer covering from a fruit or a vegetable
5	take in	_g_	e	to cut into pieces
6	eat out	_b_	f	to fall
7	chop up	_e_	g	to make something smaller
8	come down	_f_	h	to remove from somewhere or something
9	peel off	_d_	i	to stop doing something
10	take out	_h_	j	to turn bad

9 Complete the sentences with the correct form of the phrasal verbs from 8.

1 _Peel off_ the outside of the banana before you eat it.
2 If you _come across_ any unusual spices in India, will you get me some?
3 This dress is large, so I'll have to _take_ it _in_ a bit.
4 The couple _broke off_ their conversation when the waiter came to their table.
5 The meat has _gone off_. It smells disgusting!
6 I always used to _chop up_ the vegetables and my little sister would lay the table.
7 My doctor warned me that I had to _cut down_ on fattening foods.
8 I used to _eat out_ at restaurants before I got married.
9 Could you _take_ the pie _out_ of the oven, please?
10 I think I'll wait for the prices to _come down_ in the sales before I buy a new cooker.

Exam Practice

Sentence transformation

10 Complete the second sentence so that it has a similar meaning to the first sentence, using the word given. Do not change the word given. You must use between two and five words.

1. It wasn't difficult for me to stick to my diet.
   piece
   Sticking to my diet _was a piece of_ cake.
2. Stella and Wanda started baking biscuits at 9 am and they finished at 11 am.
   baking
   Stella and Wanda _were baking biscuits_ from 9 am to 11 am.
3. My brother watched a lot of TV when he was younger.
   potato
   My brother _was a couch potato_ when he was younger.
4. We arrived for dinner. Sue was asleep.
   sleeping
   Sue _was sleeping when_ we arrived for dinner.
5. Kevin was in the shower. Someone knocked on his door.
   having
   Kevin _was having a shower when_ someone knocked on his door.
6. My uncle is a very important person in that restaurant.
   big
   My uncle is a _big cheese_ in that restaurant.
7. Those two are twins, but they are very different.
   like
   Those two are twins, but they are _like chalk and_ cheese.
8. You know where the chocolates are – tell me, Mandy!
   spill
   You know where the chocolates are – _spill the beans_, Mandy!

Word formation

11 Use the word in capitals to form a word that fits in the gap.

1. I'm very _hungry_ because I didn't have breakfast. **HUNGER**
2. Add the rice to the _boiling_ water and cook for 15 minutes or so. **BOIL**
3. Do you prefer sweet pies to _savoury_ ones? **SAVOUR**
4. My mother always prepared delicious, _nutritious_ meals for her family. **NUTRITION**
5. Don't touch that _cooker_; it's very hot. **COOK**
6. No ice cream for me, thanks. I'm watching my _weight_. **WEIGH**
7. These burgers are _tasteless_! Didn't you use any spices at all? **TASTE**
8. I think I'll have the shrimp cocktail as a(n) _starter_. **START**

What Do You Think?

Speaking

12 Discuss these questions with a partner:
- What did you eat for breakfast this morning?
- What did you have for dinner last night? Who cooked it? What were you doing while he/she was cooking it?
- When did you eat out last? What was the restaurant like? What was happening while you were eating your meal?
- Did people eat healthier in the past?

Unit 4

Awareness

1 Which of these sentences are correct (C) and incorrect (I)?

1. He isn't use to eating late in the evening. — *I*
2. Our dog would to bury bones in the garden. — *I*
3. My grandmother is used to prepare a family meal every Sunday. — *I*
4. Fruit and vegetables used to be tastier. — *C*
5. Did you used to like olives when you were young? — *I*
6. Bob and Sue are getting used to how their new cooker works. — *C*
7. I didn't use to enjoy cooking, but now I do. — *C*
8. We are used to eating a big breakfast? — *I*
9. Did she use to bake her own bread in the past? — *C*
10. Was she used to eating fast food when she lived on her own? — *C*

How many did you get right?

Grammar

Used To & Would

We use *used to* + bare infinitive for
• actions that we did regularly in the past, but that we don't do now.
*My family **used to have** big family dinners when I was young.*
• states that existed in the past, but that don't exist now.
*She **used to enjoy** cooking, but now she prefers buying ready-made food.*

We use *would* + bare infinitive for actions that we did regularly in the past, but that we don't do now. We don't use it for past states.
*The chef **would prepare** his speciality every Saturday evening.*

Be Used To & Get Used To

We use *be used to* + gerund/noun to talk about something that is usual or familiar.
*My son **is used to cooking** for himself.*

We use *get used to* + gerund/noun to talk about the process of something becoming familiar.
*We **are getting used to spicy food**. We quite like it.*

Note

Be and *get* change depending on the tense that is needed in the context.

*She's **used to walking** to school.*
*Jamie **has never got used to eating** a lot of fresh produce.*

Grammar Exercises

2 Tick the sentences where used to + main verb can replace the Past Simple. Then rewrite the sentences you have ticked.

1 He ate out a lot when he was at university. ✓
   He used to eat out a lot when he was at university.

2 I lived on my own. ✓
   I used to live on my own.

3 He changed schools last year. ☐

4 We went to lots of restaurants when we were younger. ✓
   We used to go to lots of restaurants when we were younger.

5 They arrived in London an hour ago. ☐

6 Julie had lots of friends when she was a student. ✓
   Julie used to have lots of friends when she was a student.

7 I studied hard when I was taking the cooking course. ✓
   I used to study hard when I was taking the cooking course.

8 Dean and Ann spent their holidays in Greece last summer. ☐

3 Complete the sentences with the correct form of used to and the verbs in brackets.

1 They _used to go_ (go) out to a restaurant every weekend, but they don't any more.
2 I _didn't use to grow_ (not grow) vegetables, but now I grow some every summer.
3 My aunt _used to drink_ (drink) a lot of cola, but now she prefers to drink juice.
4 _Did you use to make_ (you / make) your own meals?
5 Sheila and I _didn't use to like_ (not like) each other, but now we're best friends.
6 My mother _used to cook_ (cook) dinner every night, but now she doesn't.
7 We _used to live_ (live) in a huge house, but now we live in a tiny flat.
8 I _didn't use to eat_ (not eat) fruit, but now I eat some every day.

Unit 4 21

Unit 4

4 a Rewrite the sentences using **used to** or **didn't use to**.

1 I have red hair now.
   I didn't use to have red hair.

2 I study a lot now.
   I didn't use to study a lot.

3 I have a part-time job now.
   I didn't use to have a part-time job.

4 I have a dog now.
   I didn't use to have a dog.

5 I don't wear glasses now.
   I used to wear glasses.

6 I live in the city centre now.
   I didn't use to live in the city centre.

b In which of the sentences in 4a could you also use **would**?
   2, 5

5 Complete the sentences with **used to** and/or **would**.

1 They ___used to___ live in a block of flats.
2 While on the island, she ___used to / would___ jog on the beach in the mornings.
3 He ___used to / would___ take the bus home after school.
4 We ___used to / would___ have picnics on nice summer days.
5 Katie ___used to___ have long blonde hair.
6 When we were children, we ___used to / would___ help pick the olives.
7 My parents ___used to___ have a cat named Cupcake.
8 My grandmother's baked bread ___used to___ smell fantastic.

6 Chan moved to another country to go to university. He didn't like it at first, but he is slowly getting used to his new life. Use the prompts to write sentences about Chan.

1 live in the city centre ✓
   Chan wasn't used to living in the city centre, but he is used to it now.

2 live by himself ✗
   Chan hasn't got used to living by himself.

3 be away from his parents ✗
   Chan hasn't got used to being away from his parents.

4 speak English all the time ✓
   Chan wasn't used to speaking English all the time, but he is used to it now.

5 cook his own meals ✓
   Chan wasn't used to cooking his own meals, but he is used to it now.

6 the new culture ✓
   Chan wasn't used to the new culture, but he is used to it now.

7 drive on the left side of the road ✗
   Chan hasn't got used to driving on the left side of the road.

8 rainy weather ✗
   Chan hasn't got used to rainy weather.

7 Choose the correct answers.

1 'Pat looks different now.'
   'Yes. She __ to have short black hair, didn't she?'
   a would
   b is used
   c used

2 'I've never used this cooker before.'
   'Don't worry; you'll soon __ to it.'
   a get used
   b be used
   c used

3 '__ work in that restaurant?'
   'No, he worked at one in Covent Garden.'
   a Did Tom get use to
   b Did Tom use to
   c Did Tom used to

4 Theresa __ getting up early in the mornings.
   a wouldn't
   b didn't use to
   c isn't used to

5 My brother couldn't use the program at first, but he __ to it.
   a used to
   b got used
   c got use

6 'How is your daughter, Helen?'
   'She's fine. She __ to life in the big city.'
   a got use
   b is getting used
   c used

7 'Do you remember bedtimes when we were young?'
   'Yes! Mum __ always tell us a story.'
   a was used to
   b would
   c got used to

8 Grant __ have a dog.
   a didn't use to
   b didn't use
   c didn't used to

Vocabulary

Word formation

8 Complete the table.

noun	verb	adjective
(1) _colour_	colour	coloured/colourful
taste	taste	(2) _tasty/tasteful_ /tasteless
(3) _tradition_	–	traditional
(4) _decision_	decide	decisive
choice	(5) _choose_	choosy
(6) custom/ _customer_	–	customary
(7) _mixture_	mix	mixed/mixing
(8) _trend_	–	trendy
bright	(9) _brighten_	brightly
variety	vary	(10) _various_

9 Complete the sentences with words from the table in 8.

1 What a nice old restaurant! Reds, yellows, dark blues – it's so _colourful_!
2 There were a lot of _customers_ queuing to get into *The Hummingbird Bakery*.
3 Look at all those different cakes! We're spoiled for _choice_.
4 They left the dark street and entered the _brightly_-lit restaurant.
5 Hot dogs are a(n) _traditional_ snack served at American baseball games.
6 Can I have another biscuit, please? They're very _tasty_.
7 I know there's a lot on the menu, Jan, but you need to make a(n) _decision_.
8 That new café might be modern and _trendy_, but they make terrible coffee!
9 There was such a(n) _variety_ of produce on display that she didn't know what to buy.
10 My birthday cake was a wonderful _mixture_ of vanilla and chocolate.

Unit 4

Exam Practice

Open cloze

10 Complete the sentences with the word that best fits in the gap.
1. Did your grandfather ____use____ to grow olives?
2. My dad ____would____ come home, sit at the table and have his dinner.
3. The food is a bit strange here, but I think I'm slowly ____getting____ used to it.
4. Sarah isn't used ____to____ eating spicy food, so I'm not sure she'll like these tacos.
5. We always ____used____ to cook a big turkey during the holidays.
6. ____Were____ you used to eating late when you lived in the city?
7. We did ____not____ use to eat meat, but we do now.
8. Sheila and Tim ____are____ used to having a big breakfast on Sunday mornings.

Cloze

11 Choose the correct answers.
1. Dad was ___ the meat on the BBQ outside when it started to rain.
   a frying   **b grilling**   c boiling
2. I'm very ___. Can I have a glass of water, please?
   a thirsty   b hungry   c starving
3. I'm not very hungry, so I'll just have some ___ for my breakfast.
   a vitamin   b protein   **c cereal**
4. I'd like something sweet. Let's order something for ___.
   a dessert   b starter   c course
5. Tony, that was a ___ meal – you're an amazing cook!
   a savoury   b burnt   **c delicious**
6. The service was excellent, so leave the waiter a big ___.
   a dish   **b tip**   c cooker
7. The plates and glasses are on the table; all we need now is the ___.
   a cutlery   b jugs   c bowls
8. Here, you can use this big spoon to ___ the soup.
   a chop   b peel   **c stir**

What Do You Think?

Writing

12 Read the writing task below and write the review in your notebook. Try to use lots of adjectives (in the correct order) to make your writing more appealing to the reader.

You and your friends went to a trendy restaurant in your town at the weekend and you were very happy with the meal. Write a review of the restaurant for your school newspaper giving your opinion about it and saying why you would recommend it to others.

Grammar

1 Complete the sentences with the correct form of the Present Simple or Present Continuous of the verbs in brackets.

1. Dad ___is seeing___ (see) a doctor about his headaches this afternoon at two o'clock.
2. Billy can't come to the phone because he ___'s studying___ (study). He ___studies___ (study) every evening at this time.
3. ___Do they usually call___ (they / usually / call) you before they come to your house?
4. Linda ___is jogging___ (jog) in the park at the moment. She ___jogs___ (jog) every morning before she ___has___ (have) breakfast.
5. My family ___gets___ (get) an email from my cousin, Jane, once a week. She ___'s cycling___ (cycle) around France and ___always remembers___ (always remember) to email us.
6. Cindy ___finds___ (find) maths very difficult. She ___doesn't seem___ (not seem) to be able to do even simple equations.
7. Look! It ___'s snowing___ (snow). It ___rarely snows___ (rarely snow) in Scotland at this time of the year.
8. When I ___do___ (do) well in school, I ___feel___ (feel) very proud.
9. My grandparents ___are staying___ (stay) with us tonight.
10. My mother ___is forever complaining___ (forever complain) about how loud I play music.

2 Complete the sentences with the word that best fits each gap.

1. I'm hungry. I think I'll make ___a___ sandwich.
2. I want to make a pie, so I'll need ___some___ flour and eggs.
3. She has a problem. Can you give her ___some___ advice?
4. Can I have ___an___ apple, please?
5. We're all out of milk, so I'll go buy ___some___.
6. It's Saturday! I've got ___lots___ of time to do whatever I want.
7. That music ___is___ giving me a headache! Turn it off!
8. How ___many___ people were at your family get-together last weekend?
9. There isn't ___any___ food in the fridge; it's completely empty!
10. Could I have a ___little___ sugar for my tea, please?

3 Circle the correct words.

1. (Were you cooking) / Did you cook when your husband arrived home?
2. The cook (stirred) / was stirring the mixture, tasted it and added a bit of salt.
3. (Did they go) / Were they going to that new restaurant last Sunday?
4. I wasn't having / (didn't have) time for lunch today!
5. My brother (didn't get) / wasn't getting here an hour ago; he's been here all morning.
6. Dad watered / (was watering) the garden while Mum was washing the car.
7. Kevin (was chopping) / chopped onions when he cut his hand.
8. The sun (was shining) / shone and the children were playing happily in the park.
9. I (believed) / was believing him when he said he'd pay for the meal.
10. Jan was never eating / (never ate) in the school canteen when she was a student.

Review 1

4 Choose the correct answers.

1 Kevin looks different. He ___ have red hair and now it's blond!
   a would
   b used to

2 'I've never used this computer program before.'
   'It's easy; you'll soon ___ to it.'
   a used
   b get used

3 '___ be a chef at Chez Canard?'
   'No, he didn't, but my uncle did.'
   a Did your father use to
   b Did your father get used to

4 I know that man. He ___ to teach me maths at school.
   a would
   b used

5 William ___ getting up late in the mornings – he's an early riser.
   a isn't used to
   b didn't use to

6 My grandmother couldn't use the new cooker at first, but she ___ to it.
   a used
   b got used

7 'How is Tony doing at his new school?'
   'Very well! He is slowly ___ it.'
   a getting used to
   b being used to

8 'Do you remember weekends at Grandma and Grandpa's?'
   'Yes! Grandma ___ always make us tasty breakfasts.'
   a was used to
   b would

9 My sister ___ live by herself, but she does now.
   a isn't getting used to
   b didn't use to

10 We ___ have a pet, but now we've got a cat.
   a didn't use to
   b didn't used to

5 Circle the correct words.

1 Mum is always making / **always makes** lunch at twelve o'clock on Sundays.
2 My father got used to / **used to** work in a restaurant when he was younger.
3 Celia likes a few / **a little** honey in her tea.
4 What time **does the film start** / is the filming starting this evening?
5 Could I have **a glass** / loaf of milk, please?
6 We went into the garden and we **had** / were having a barbecue.
7 They were eating breakfast while / **when** the phone rang.
8 My grandfather is speaking / **speaks** three languages.
9 Tim is never getting used to / **has never got used to** the smell of onions.
10 Are there **any** / some biscuits in the cupboard?

6 Find the mistakes and correct the sentences where necessary. Put a tick (✓) below those which do not need correcting.

1 My cousin Jim stays with us for the time being.
   My cousin Jim is staying with us for the time being.

2 I expect you enjoyed the dinner party last night.
   ✓

3 Would you like some orange, Billy?
   Would you like an orange, Billy?

4 Look! The dog's feet is very big!
   Look! The dog's feet are very big!

5 Peter visits his Aunt Kate twice a month.
   ✓

6 There wasn't many rain last summer.
   There wasn't much rain last summer.

7 Was the farmer working in his field all day?
   ✓

Use of English

Sentence transformation

7 Complete the second sentence so that it has a similar meaning to the first sentence, using the word given. Do not change the word given. You must use between two and five words.

1 My cousin played a lot of sports when he was younger.
  to
  My cousin _____used to play_____ a lot of sports when he was younger.

2 Dad would never read the paper before dinner in the evenings.
  to
  Dad _____didn't use to_____ read the paper before dinner in the evenings.

3 Grant has an appointment to see his lawyer on Friday.
  is
  Grant _____is seeing_____ his lawyer on Friday.

4 Vaughn has just moved to the city, so he finds it quite strange.
  used
  Vaughn _____isn't used to_____ living in the city.

5 Shall I put milk in your tea?
  some
  Would you _____like some milk_____ in your tea?

6 I wonder if this restaurant serves vegetarian dishes.
  any
  I wonder if there _____are any vegetarian dishes_____ on the menu in this restaurant.

7 Our teacher complains about our work all the time.
  continually
  Our teacher _____is continually complaining_____ about our work.

8 I haven't got much spare time to spend with you today.
  a
  I've only got _____a little time_____ to spend with you today.

9 Tommy started to work on his project at 7 pm and he finished at 10 pm.
  working
  Tommy _____was working on his project_____ from 7 pm to 10 pm.

10 They turned up for lunch. Mum was asleep.
   sleeping
   Mum _____was sleeping when_____ they turned up for lunch.

Word formation

8 Use the word in capitals to form a word that fits in the gap.

1 Look at that fruit and vegetable display; isn't it lovely and _____colourful_____? **COLOUR**
2 This soup is very _____tasty_____, Martha. You're an amazing cook. **TASTE**
3 I prefer *Mario's Bistro* to *Le Chateau* because there's more _____variety_____ on the menu. **VARY**
4 Here at *Good Eats*, we offer both _____savoury_____ and sweet pies. **SAVOUR**
5 I've gained a lot of _____weight_____ recently; I need to go on a diet. **WEIGH**
6 This cereal is both delicious and _____nutritious_____. **NUTRITION**
7 I love all my _____relatives_____, but I think Aunt Faye is my favourite. **RELATE**
8 You're an hour late again! You're the most _____unreliable_____ person I know! **RELY**

Review 1

Grammar

9 For questions 1–10, choose the word or phrase that best completes the sentence.

1 Why ___ eating with your mouth open? It's disgusting!
  A always are you
  B you do always
  (C) are you always

2 How ___ pieces of cake do you want?
  A much
  B some
  (C) many

3 What time ___ on TV tonight, Dad?
  (A) does Master Chef start
  B is Master Chef starting
  C did Master Chef start

4 We were making sandwiches when we ___ there weren't any tomatoes.
  A are realising
  (B) realised
  C were realising

5 Charlie ___ to the dentist yesterday.
  A was going
  B is going
  (C) went

6 I ___ of making spaghetti for lunch this Sunday; what do you think?
  (A) am thinking
  B think
  C thought

7 My aunt and uncle ___ with us at the moment.
  A stayed
  (B) are staying
  C stay

8 My friend Bonnie ___ got three brothers.
  (A) has
  B is having
  C was having

9 Grandma ___ to live alone, but she does now.
  (A) didn't use
  B wasn't used
  C isn't used

10 We found ___ information about twins on the Internet.
  A an
  B much
  (C) the

Vocabulary

10 For questions 11–20, choose the word or phrase that best completes the sentence.

11 I want to ___ a really big family when I get older.
  A get
  (B) have
  C do

12 My older brother is ___ married next week.
  A keeping
  B having
  (C) getting

13 I'm not telling you because you can't ___ a secret!
  A have
  B do
  (C) keep

14 The couple ___ the chef a compliment on his great cooking.
  A had
  (B) paid
  C did

15 Peel the potatoes and ___ them in lots of salted water for ten minutes.
  A fry
  (B) boil
  C grill

16 I didn't think Bob and Marge would ever ___, but it seems they have.
  (A) break up
  B bring up
  C come down

17 That dress is a bit large. It needs to be ___.
  A moved in
  B passed down
  (C) taken in

18 You eat too much fattening food; you need to ___.
  A go off
  (B) cut down
  C turn to

19 Let's take a look ___ what happens at an Italian wedding.
  (A) at
  B in
  C up

20 All the friends ___ the bride were at a big party last night.
  A for
  B with
  (C) of

28

Unit 5

Awareness

1 Which of these sentences are correct (C) and incorrect (I)?

1 Man has been damaging the environment for centuries! — C
2 Experts have discovered a new kind of insect in December. — I
3 The zoo just closed for the day. — I
4 Has she been recycling her rubbish for a long time? — C
5 They have been conducting research on the reef since 2004. — C
6 We haven't been living here since five years. — I
7 I have studied endangered marine species last year. — I
8 How long have you been travelling in Africa? — C
9 Dr Fossey has been to Rwanda; she'll be back next month. — I
10 We have had five terrible storms so far this winter. — C

How many did you get right?

Grammar

Present Perfect Simple

Affirmative	Negative	Questions
I/we/you/they **have** (**'ve**) look**ed** he/she/it **has** (**'s**) look**ed**	I/we/you/they **have not** (**haven't**) look**ed** he/she/it **has not** (**hasn't**) look**ed**	**Have** I/we/you/they look**ed**? **Has** he/she/it look**ed**?
Short Answers		
Yes, I/we/you/they look**ed**. **Yes**, he/she/it look**ed**.	**No**, I/we/you/they **haven't**. **No**, he/she/it **hasn't**.	

Spelling: talk → talk**ed**, place → plac**ed**, travel → trave**lled**, ti**dy** → ti**died**, stay → stay**ed**

We use the Present Perfect Simple for
• something that started in the past and has continued until now.
*That biologist **has worked** in the Amazon since 2003.*
• something that happened in the past, but we don't know or we don't say exactly when.
*Ecologists **have discovered** a new problem.*
• something that happened in the past and has a result that affects the present.
*Illegal hunting **has endangered** many species on the planet.*
• actions that have just finished.
*The fisherman **has just caught** a fish.*
• experiences and achievements.
*The scientist **has won** many awards.*

> **Note**
> Some verbs are irregular and do not follow these spelling rules. See a list of irregular verbs on pages 156-157.

> **Note**
> Some common time expressions that are often used with the Present Perfect Simple are *already, ever, for, for a long time/ages, just, never, once, recently, since 2007/June, so far, twice, three times, until now, yet*, etc.
> *Dr Goodwall has worked with apes **since 2005**.*

Have Been & Have Gone

Notice the difference between *have been* and *have gone*.
have been = someone has gone somewhere and has now returned
*We **have been** to the Great Barrier Reef. It's amazing!*
have gone = someone has gone somewhere and is still there
*Peter is not here. He **has gone** to the museum.*

Ago, For & Since

We often use *ago* with the Past Simple, and *for* and *since* with the Present Perfect Simple.
We use *ago* at the end of a sentence with the Past Simple.
*I went to Australia two weeks **ago**.*

Unit 5

We use *for* with an expression that shows a period of time at the end of a sentence with the Present Perfect Simple.
*Dinosaurs have been extinct **for** ages.*

We use *since* with a point of time in the past at the end of a sentence with the Present Perfect Simple.
*Tony has been a scientist **since** 2005.*

Present Perfect Simple & Past Simple

We use the Present Perfect Simple when we talk about something that happened in the past and has a result that affects the present. We also use the Present Perfect Simple when we don't know or we don't say when something happened in the past. We use the Past Simple when we say when something happened.
*The use of air conditioners **has increased** global warming.*
*She **has travelled** all over the world.*
*They **visited** the Galapagos Islands last year.*

Present Perfect Continuous

Affirmative	Negative	Questions
I/we/you/they **have** ('ve) **been** look**ing**	I/we/you/they **have not** (**haven't**) **been** look**ing**	**Have** I/we/you/they **been** look**ing**?
he/she/it **has** ('s) **been** look**ing**	he/she/it **has not** (**hasn't**) **been** look**ing**	**Has** he/she/it **been** look**ing**?
Short Answers		
Yes, I/we/you/they **have**. **Yes**, he/she/it **has**.	**No**, I/we/you/they **haven't**. **No**, he/she/it **hasn't**.	

Spelling: tak**e** → tak**ing**, swim → swim**ming**, stud**y** → stud**ying**

We use the Present Perfect Continuous
• for actions that started in the past and are still in progress now or have happened repeatedly until now.
*The team of experts **has been looking** for rare butterflies in Borneo.*
• for actions that happened repeatedly in the past and have finished recently, but that have results that affect the present.
*My head hurts because I **have been studying** for hours.*
• to emphasise how long actions have been in progress for.
*My uncle **has been exploring** caves for 20 years.*

> **Note:** Some common time expressions that are often used with the Present Perfect Continuous are *all day/night/week, for years / a long time / ages, lately, recently, since*. We can use *How long ...?* with the Present Perfect Continuous in questions and *for (very) long* in questions and negative sentences.
>
> *I have been working on this science project **all day**.*
> ***How long** has Martha been working as a biologist?*
> *We haven't been searching for new species **for very long**. It's only been three months.*

Present Perfect Simple & Present Perfect Continuous

We use the Present Perfect Simple to talk about something we have done or achieved, or an action that is complete. It is also used to say how many times something happened.
*She **has read** that science journal three times in the last week.*

We use the Present Perfect Continuous to talk about how long something has been happening. It is not important whether or not it has finished.
*The conversation **has been going** on for hours.*

Grammar Exercises

2 Complete the sentences with the correct form of the Past Simple or Present Perfect Simple of the verbs in brackets.

1. A: _Have you seen_ (you / see) Dr Stevens?
   B: Actually, she _'s just left_ (just leave).
2. A: I _haven't felt_ (not feel) well since I got back from Africa.
   B: Well, _have you seen_ (you / see) a doctor yet?
3. A: _Have you had_ (you / have) any news from Maria?
   B: As a matter of fact, she _called_ (call) me from Brazil yesterday.
4. A: Peter _has bought_ (buy) new snorkelling equipment, hasn't he?
   B: Yes, he _bought_ (buy) a new mask and snorkel last week.
5. A: _Has she sent_ (she / send) the donation to *Greenpeace* yet?
   B: Yes, she _posted_ (post) a cheque this morning.
6. A: _Have they talked_ (they / talk) to the science professor?
   B: Yes, they _talked_ (talk) to her last night.
7. A: How long _has Petra worked_ (Petra / work) as a zoologist?
   B: She _'s worked_ (work) as a zoologist for five years.
8. A: _Have they visited_ (they / visit) Australia?
   B: Many times. In fact, they _went_ (go) in January.

3 Use the prompts to write sentences. Use the Present Perfect Simple.

1. I / already / see / the fossils
   I have already seen the fossils.
2. Tina / move / house / yet?
   Has Tina moved house yet?
3. we / already / catch / eight fish / today
   We've already caught eight fish today.
4. Jack / never / travel / abroad
   Jack has never travelled abroad.
5. the boat / just / arrive / at the port
   The boat has just arrived at the port.
6. you / ever / meet / any famous scientists?
   Have you ever met any famous scientists?
7. she / try / snorkelling?
   Has she tried snorkelling?
8. they / not finish / their research / yet
   They haven't finished their research yet.

4 Complete the sentences with have/has been or have/has gone.

1. We _'ve been_ to Sydney three times so far this year, but we want to go back again.
2. You can't see Sam before Sunday. He _'s gone_ on a digging expedition.
3. Martha _has been_ to the Cliffs of Dover many times.
4. Ken and Tina _have gone_ to Argentina for a few weeks. They're coming back tomorrow.
5. Grant _has gone_ to the library. He should be back by noon.
6. The biologist _has gone_ to the research centre in the jungle and won't be back for hours.
7. I _'ve been_ to the museum twice this week.
8. Tony and Ben aren't here right now. They _'ve gone_ into town for supplies.

Unit 5

5 Circle the correct words.

1 They haven't reached the top of the mountain ever / **yet**.
2 Have you for / **just** arrived?
3 The panda has yet / **already** had its injections.
4 It hasn't rained in Tanzania just / **for** months.
5 We became interested in endangered species three years **ago** / already.
6 He hasn't been to the rainforest for / **since** last year.
7 Has Paul yet / **ever** heard the professor speak?
8 I haven't talked to my brother since / **for** weeks.

6 Complete the sentences with the correct form of the Present Perfect Simple or Present Perfect Continuous of the verbs in brackets.

1 **A:** You look terrible, Janet!
   B: I know. I _haven't been feeling_ (not feel) well recently.
2 **A:** Is Fran down by the pond?
   B: Yes, she _'s been watching_ (watch) the frogs all morning.
3 **A:** Do you like Professor Cookson?
   B: Oh yes! She's one of the most intelligent people I _'ve ever met_ (ever meet).
4 **A:** Are you still working on your project?
   B: No, I _'ve just finished_ (just finish) it.
5 **A:** Your English is very good.
   B: Thank you. I _'ve been learning_ (learn) English since I was very young.
6 **A:** How long _have you been digging_ (you / dig) in the garden?
   B: For three hours now.
7 **A:** Are Dean and Ann still here?
   B: No, they _'ve already left_ (already leave).
8 **A:** Is this your first visit to the rainforest?
   B: Yes, we _'ve never been_ (never be) here before.

7 Find the mistakes and correct the sentences.

1 Have they ever see a Giant Panda?
   Have they ever seen a Giant Panda?
2 Lynn and I graduate last year.
   Lynn and I graduated last year.
3 We've moved to this city five years ago.
   We moved to this city five years ago.
4 Nancy is lived in Peru for two months now.
   Nancy has lived/has been living in Peru for two months now.
5 They've make a lot of mistakes.
   They made a lot of mistakes.
6 The ecologist has went to look at the stream.
   The ecologist has gone to look at the stream.
7 Jake hasn't finished his research just.
   Jack hasn't finished his research yet.
8 I did already done my science homework.
   I've already done my science homework.
9 The biologist has just came back from the glacier.
   The biologist has just come back from the glacier.
10 Have you ever travel to Antarctica?
   Have you ever travelled to Antarctica?

Vocabulary

Prepositions

8 Choose the correct answers.

1 ___ years of something
   a (after)
   b across
2 raise awareness ___ something
   a around
   b (about)
3 for ___ 20 years
   a between
   b (over)
4 stretch from somewhere ___ somewhere else
   a in
   b (to)
5 everything ___ something to something else
   a (from)
   b for
6 show up ___ something
   a (in)
   b over
7 make their way ___ something
   a at
   b (onto)
8 ___ the moment
   a (at)
   b on
9 turn ___ something
   a instead of
   b (into)
10 ___ something happens
   a (before)
   b during

9 Complete the sentences with the correct form of the prepositions from 8.

1 Governments must do something about pollution ____before____ it's too late.
2 They have been conducting their research for ____over____ a decade now.
3 In Australia, you can do everything ____from____ snorkelling to scuba diving!
4 They want to turn the coastal area ____into____ a golf course.
5 The landfill site stretched from the edge of town ____to____ the banks of the river.
6 Deadly poisons have been showing up ____in____ many species of fish.
7 ____After____ months of hard work, we've finally managed to clean up the city's parks.
8 Greenpeace has been campaigning to raise awareness ____about____ seal hunting.
9 Produce sprayed with pesticides can make its way ____onto____ our dinner tables.
10 I can't talk right now; I'm very busy ____at____ the moment.

Exam Practice

Cloze

10 Choose the correct answers.

1 They believe the hikers entered the dark ___ and got lost.
   a cliff   b (cave)   c stream
2 The world's ___ are melting at an alarming rate.
   a (glaciers)   b valleys   c threats
3 We can get cold fresh water from that ___.
   a pond   b (stream)   c planet
4 From the top of the mountain, we had a fantastic view of the ___ below.
   a energy   b warming   c (valley)
5 The ___ is under threat from illegal logging.
   a (rainforest)   b cliff   c fuels
6 My dream is to live in a lighthouse on the ___ of Scotland.
   a stream   b cave   c (coast)
7 Don't go too near the edge of the ___; it's very dangerous.
   a habitat   b (cliff)   c species
8 ___ energy comes from the sun.
   a Fossil   b Fuel   c (Solar)

Unit 5 **33**

Unit 5

Word formation

11 Use the word in capitals to form a word that fits in the gap.

1 We can get _____renewable_____ energy from the sun, the wind and water. — **RENEW**
2 Have they come up with any ideas about how to slow down _____global_____ warming? — **GLOBE**
3 _____Organic_____ food may be a bit more expensive, but I'm sure it's healthier. — **ORGAN**
4 The list of _____endangered_____ species on the planet gets longer every day. — **DANGER**
5 The _____natural_____ habitat of this lizard is the rainforests of South America. — **NATURE**
6 We need to set up more _____conservation_____ areas to keep animals safe. — **CONSERVE**
7 I've been reading about the _____destruction_____ of the rainforest; it's terrible! — **DESTROY**
8 So many species face _____extinction_____ these days; we really have to do something. — **EXTINCT**

What Do You Think?

Speaking

12 Talk to your partner about:

- two things you have/haven't done this week.
- one thing you've done to help the planet.
- two things you've been doing for the past few years that have been good for the environment.

Unit 6

Awareness

1 Which of these sentences are correct (C) and incorrect (I)?

1. Can Tony play a piano? __I__
2. Jake is in hospital; he might get out tomorrow. __C__
3. The zoo bought an ostrich. The ostrich is very big. __C__
4. The Pindus Mountains are located in Europe. __C__
5. The Greeks are very proud of their history. __C__
6. Do you have to wear an uniform to work? __I__
7. The scientists have a meeting once the week. __I__
8. He is a best zoologist in the country. __I__
9. A sun rises in the east and sets in the west. __I__
10. A lot of people have dinner in the evening. __C__

How many did you get right? ☐

Grammar

The Indefinite Article: A/An

We use *a* before a consonant sound.
a gorilla
a unicorn

We use *an* before a vowel sound.
an aeroplane
an hour

We use *a/an*
• with singular countable nouns.
*She always has **a** book with her.*
• to mean per/each in expressions of frequency.
*The biologists meet once **a** month.*
• to mention something for the first time.
(When we continue talking about it we use *the*.)
***An** eagle has made a nest in that tree.*
***The** eagle has laid two eggs.*
• to show job, status, etc.
*She is **an** ecologist.*

The Definite Article: The

We use *the* with singular and plural countable nouns and uncountable nouns to talk about something specific when the noun is mentioned for a second time.
*Look! There's a cat on **a** sofa. **The** sofa looks rather dirty.*

We also use *the* before
• unique nouns.
***The** earth is round and it orbits **the** sun.*
• names of cinemas, theatres, ships, hotels, etc.
*Where was **the** Titanic built?*
*They're staying at **the** Strand Hotel in London.*
• names of rivers, deserts, mountain ranges, and names or nouns with *of*.
*Where is **the** Gobi Desert?*
***The** Rockies are popular with skiers.*
***The** King of Norway is on an official visit.*
• countries or groups of countries whose names are plural.
*Is **the** United States bigger than Canada?*
*We come from **the** Bahamas.*
• musical instruments.
*Carol plays **the** guitar and **the** banjo.*

Unit 6 35

Unit 6

- nationalities.

The Scottish are well-known for their story-telling.
The Japanese have an interesting culture.

- adjectives used as nouns.

The rich should help the poor.

- superlatives.

The cheetah is the fastest animal on the planet.

- the following words: *beach, countryside, station, jungle,* etc.

It's not warm enough to go to the beach today.

- *morning, afternoon, evening.*

Many people go to work in the morning.

We do not use *the* before
- proper nouns.

Is Jimmy at school today?

- names of sports, games, colours, days, months, drinks, holidays, meals and languages (not followed by the word *language*).

Yellow is my mother's favourite colour.

- subjects of study.

I find maths very difficult.

- names of countries, cities, streets (BUT: **the** *High Street*), squares, bridges (BUT: **the** *Golden Gate Bridge*), parks, stations, individual mountains, islands, lakes, continents.

Glasgow is a large city in Scotland.

- *bed, church, school, hospital, prison, university, college, court* when we talk about something related to the main purpose of the place. (*Work* never takes *the*.)

Kevin is in prison. (He committed a crime and is an inmate there.)
Pam has gone to the prison to visit Kevin. (She's not an inmate; she's gone to visit someone.)

- means of transportation in expressions like *by plane,* etc. (BUT: *on the plane*).

We decided to go to Australia by ship.

Grammar Exercises

2 **Write a or an.**

1. _a_ collection
2. _an_ hour
3. _an_ onion
4. _an_ alarm clock
5. _an_ umbrella
6. _a_ uniform
7. _a_ reef
8. _a_ house
9. _an_ airport
10. _a_ fish

3 **Complete the sentences with a, an or the.**

1. _The_ group gets together twice _a_ month to discuss conservation.
2. _The_ president of the college is also _an_ anthropologist.
3. Aunt Edna has gone to _the_ school to pick up Joey.
4. I saw _an_ octopus in the sea. _The_ octopus had eight 'arms'.
5. I think I'll go up to _the_ High Street because I need _a_ new umbrella.
6. _The_ moon is round and it orbits _the_ earth.
7. _A_ friend of mine is staying at _the_ Hilton while he's in France.
8. Everyone should do their part to help _the_ poor.

4 Circle the correct words.

1 The biology / **Biology** is my brother's favourite subject.
2 Does that archaeologist come from Philippines / **the Philippines**?
3 What time do you usually eat the breakfast / **breakfast**?
4 Has anyone ever managed to climb the Mount Etna / **Mount Etna**?
5 I usually do volunteer work on the Saturday / **Saturday**.
6 Is the Professor Jones / **Professor Jones** going to the conference?
7 Did you play **football** / the football when you were a student?
8 I believe Dian Fossey was **the best** / best zoologist ever.
9 Most of the scientists will travel to Peru by **plane** / the plane.
10 A group of us are going to **the countryside** / countryside to pick up rubbish.

5 Complete the sentences with these words adding the where necessary. Use each word twice.

bed   church   hospital   prison   school

1 My grandmother goes to _____church_____ every Sunday morning.
2 Everyone is going to _____the church_____ on Elm Street for the wedding.
3 I'm going to _____bed_____; cleaning up the park was exhausting.
4 If you're looking for your snorkelling equipment, it's on _____the bed_____.
5 Is that _____the prison_____ where Oscar Wilde was a prisoner?
6 Her uncle is in _____prison_____ for being part of the anti-whaling protest.
7 Many people were injured in the crash and were taken to _____hospital_____.
8 My sister just had an operation, so I'm going to _____the hospital_____ to see her.
9 Do you think Tom will go to university once he finishes _____school_____?
10 If you're going by _____the school_____, can you pick up Giselle?

6 Complete the dialogues with a, an, the or no article (–).

1 **A:** Did you stay in __a__ hotel when you went to __–__ Athens?
   B: Yes. I had __a__ nice room in __the__ Hilton.
2 **A:** What did you have for __–__ lunch at __–__ school today?
   B: I had __an__ apple and __a__ sandwich.
3 **A:** How often do you take __a__ holiday?
   B: We go to our house in __the__ countryside twice __a__ year.
4 **A:** Did you go to __the__ Playhouse Theatre last night?
   B: Yes, it was __an__ enjoyable evening and the play was __the__ best I've ever seen.
5 **A:** Have you got __a__ car?
   B: No, but I've got __a__ bike. __The__ bike I've got is a new one.
6 **A:** That's __an__ interesting painting.
   B: Isn't it? It was painted by __an__ artist from __–__ Italy.
7 **A:** Did you enjoy your trip to __–__ Europe?
   B: Yes, and I was especially impressed with __the__ Eiffel Tower and __the__ Louvre.
8 **A:** Do you play __–__ golf?
   B: Yes, I do. I often play with __the__ president of my company.

Unit 6

7 Choose the correct answers.

1. Look at ___ lions; they are chasing a gazelle.
   a a
   b –
   c the
2. Hans and I travelled to the mountains by ___ train.
   a –
   b a
   c the
3. I have to go to ___ Covent Garden Station; I hope I don't get lost!
   a a
   b the
   c –
4. I saw ___ interesting documentary about whales last night.
   a the
   b an
   c a
5. Hurry up, Megan. We have to be there in ___ hour!
   a the
   b a
   c an
6. Did you know that ___ Prince of Wales is interested in conservation?
   a –
   b a
   c the
7. They've been following ___ Amazon River for days.
   a an
   b the
   c a
8. How long have you been studying ___ English language?
   a the
   b an
   c –

Vocabulary

Collocations & Expressions

8 Match to form collocations and expressions.

1. fight — *b*
2. bring — *a*
3. save — *c*
4. face — *h*
5. take — *d*
6. do — *f*
7. be — *g*
8. form — *e*

a attention to
b pollution
c energy
d action
e a group
f research
g on the verge of
h great danger

9 Complete the sentences with the correct form of the expressions from 8.

1. Many of the world's species ___*are on the verge of*___ extinction.
2. We can all ___*save energy*___ by turning off lights when we leave a room.
3. We must ___*bring attention to*___ what is happening to whales! If we don't help them, they will die out!
4. Factory owners can do their part to ___*fight pollution*___ by making sure toxic waste does not make its way into our rivers and streams.
5. The government must ___*take action*___ now! They must help the poor and homeless!
6. Officials ___*face great dangers*___ when they go into the jungle to catch poachers.
7. Last year, the students at my school ___*formed a group*___ called 'The Savers of the Planet'.
8. Dr Goodall is ___*doing research*___ on how deforestation is affecting the great apes.

Exam Practice

Open cloze

10 Complete the sentences with the word that best fits each gap.

1. Lonesome George was a giant tortoise that lived in _____the_____ Galapagos Islands.
2. _____After_____ years of research, the scientist made a great discovery.
3. Do you know what _____the_____ most common language on the planet is?
4. Some recycled waste can be turned _____into_____ fuel to heat our homes.
5. I read _____an_____ interesting article in the paper yesterday about camels.
6. The park has every animal you can think of, _____from_____ lambs to lions!
7. The Professor is giving a lecture _____at_____ the moment.
8. I've been playing _____the_____ piano for many years now.

Sentence transformation

11 Complete the second sentence so that it has a similar meaning to the first sentence, using the word given. Do not change the word given. You must use between two and five words.

1. We have to get people to take notice of what is happening to seals.
   bring
   We have to _____bring attention to_____ what is happening to seals.

2. We, the people of Stanton, have decided to do something about the problem of litter.
   action
   We, the people of Stanton, have decided to _____take action on_____ the problem of litter.

3. Many species are about to die out.
   on
   Many species are _____are on the verge of_____ extinction.

4. My friends and I are going to get together to fight pollution.
   form
   My friends and I are going to _____form a group_____ to fight pollution.

5. The government has to give people information on the importance of saving energy.
   raise
   The government has to _____raise awareness about_____ the importance of saving energy.

6. Dr Stevens works digging up old things in Egypt.
   archaeologist
   Dr Stevens _____is an archaeologist_____ who works in Egypt.

7. This shop sells a lot of things: clothes, toys and even books!
   from
   This shop sells everything _____from clothes to toys_____ and even books!

8. Some fish contained bits of plastic.
   showed
   Bits of plastic _____showed up in_____ some fish.

What Do You Think?

Writing

12 Read the writing task below and write the article in your notebook. Make sure you edit your work carefully after you've finished writing.

You write articles for your school newspaper. Write a short article for the newspaper about an event in your town that helped the environment.

Unit 7

Awareness

1 Which of these sentences are correct (C) and incorrect (I)?

1	My father is a man whose easy to talk to.	I
2	Spain, that is in Europe, is a beautiful city.	I
3	Where is dog who was stolen?	I
4	Friendship is a relationship which I could not live without.	C
5	My best friend who name is Joe is very reliable.	I
6	Tuesday, 2 September was the day when I met my husband.	C
7	That is the restaurant that my parents took me for my birthday.	I
8	Gina is a person that never lies.	C
9	Jake, who lives next door to me, used to be my boyfriend.	C
10	That's the building where my mother used to work.	C

How many did you get right? ☐

Grammar
Relative Clauses

Relative clauses give more information about the subject or the object of a sentence. They are introduced by the following words (relative pronouns):
- *who* for people.
*The film is about a girl **who** has no friends.*
- *which* for things.
*The book **which** was about sniffer dogs was fantastic.*
- *whose* to show possession.
*The orangutan **whose** name is Suryia lives in the USA.*
- *when* for time.
*An anniversary is a time **when** people celebrate.*
- *where* for places.
*This is the zoo **where** there are no cages.*

Defining Relative Clauses

This type of relative clause gives us information that we need to be able to understand who or what the speaker is talking about. We do not use commas to separate it from the rest of the sentence. We can use *that* instead of *who* and *which* in defining relative clauses.
*These are the people **who/that** help the poor and homeless.*

Non-defining Relative Clauses

This type of relative clause gives us extra information which isn't necessary to understand the meaning of the main clause. We use commas to separate it from the rest of the sentence.
*His mother, **who** is a psychologist, works with young people.*

Grammar Exercises

2 Use the prompts to write sentences. Use who, which or where.

1. mobile phone / something / we use to call friends
   A mobile phone is something which we use to call friends.
2. cinema / place / we watch films
   A cinema is a place where we watch films.
3. rescue worker / person / save people
   A rescue worker is a person who saves people.
4. clothes dryer / machine / we use to dry clothes
   A clothes dryer is a machine which we use to dry clothes.
5. zoo / place / we see animals
   A zoo is a place where we see animals.
6. teacher / person / teach young people
   A teacher is a person who teaches young people.
7. printer / machine / we use to print things from a computer
   A printer is a machine which we use to print things from a computer.
8. gorilla / animal / live in Africa
   A gorilla is an animal which lives in Africa.
9. doctor / person / make people feel better
   A doctor is a person who makes people feel better.
10. pool / place / we go swimming
    A pool is a place where we go swimming.

3 Match to form sentences.

1. Is Stella the journalist — h
2. That is the café — a
3. That is the woman — d
4. Athens is the city — f
5. I'll always remember the time — j
6. That's the school — c
7. The little girl — g
8. Is this the book — e
9. This is the kitten — i
10. This is the child — b

a which serves the best coffee on the planet!
b whose father teaches us maths.
c where I went when I was a primary student.
d whose son is my best friend.
e which you read last month?
f where you can see the Acropolis.
g who is playing with the puppy is Gillian.
h who works for *The Evening News*?
i which comes into our garden all the time.
j when my parents got me my first puppy.

4 Match to form sentences. Add the correct relative pronoun.

1. This is the cabin — b
2. Alexander Graham Bell is the man — a
3. The doctor — f
4. Agatha Christie, — g
5. We met a boy — e
6. Is that the place — h
7. The documentary — d
8. Is he the person — c

a _who/that_ invented the telephone.
b _where_ my grandfather was born.
c _who/that_ you used to have as a best friend?
d _which/that_ I saw this morning was very interesting.
e _whose_ name is Steven.
f _who/that_ looked after my sick grandmother was very kind.
g _whose_ books have been translated into many languages, was British.
h _where_ you met your girlfriend?

Unit 7 41

Unit 7

5 a Join the sentences using relative pronouns. Put commas where necessary.

1 That's the CD. My friend gave it to me.
   That's the CD which/that my friend gave to me.

2 This is the girl. Her uncle works in a zoo.
   This is the girl whose uncle works in a zoo.

3 This is the boy. He's my brother's classmate.
   This is the boy who/that is my brother's classmate.

4 That's the girl. Her mother works as a dog trainer.
   That's the girl whose mother works as a dog trainer.

5 They work in a factory. The factory makes computer games.
   They work in a factory that/which makes computer games.

6 18 September was the day. We first met.
   18 September was the day when we first met.

7 That's the woman. She got engaged last month.
   That's the woman who/that got engaged last month.

8 That's the cinema. I saw a film there on Saturday.
   That's the cinema where I saw a film on Saturday.

9 He lives in a big house. It's in the countryside.
   He lives in a big house which/that is in the countryside.

10 Ms Jones is a child psychologist. She's 42 years old.
   Ms Jones, who/that is a child psychologist, is 42 years old.

11 This is the motorbike. We got it last year.
   This is the motorbike that/which we got last year.

12 This is the man. His dog found the illegal food.
   This is the man whose dog found the illegal food.

b In which of the sentences in 5a could the relative pronouns be omitted?
   1, 6, 11

6 Complete the sentences in two different ways.

1 Sheila is playing with a girl. The girl is her sister.
   a The girl who Sheila is playing with is her sister.
   b The girl Sheila is playing with is her sister.

2 He works for a zoologist. The zoologist is very well known.
   a The zoologist who/that he works for is very well known.
   b The zoologist he works for is very well known.

3 We borrowed a ladder from the neighbours. The ladder is made of aluminium.
   a The ladder which/that we borrowed from the neighbours is made of aluminium.
   b The ladder we borrowed from the neighbours is made of aluminium.

4 Kevin has gone to a graduation party. The party is at his friend's flat.
   a The graduation party which/that Kevin has gone to is at his friend's flat.
   b The graduation party Kevin has gone to is at his friend's flat.

5 He was talking to a man. The man is his English teacher.
   a The man who/that he was talking to is his English teacher.
   b The man he was talking to is his English teacher.

6 We got married on a day. The day was sunny and hot.
   a The day when we got married was sunny and hot.
   b The day we got married was sunny and hot.

7 Complete the sentences about you. Use relative pronouns.

1 The person who I like the most is _____*Student's own answers*_____.
2 2012 was the year _____.
3 The city _____.
4 My father _____.
5 The pet _____.
6 My favourite book _____.
7 The place _____.
8 I know a woman _____.
9 The sport _____.
10 The singer _____.

Vocabulary

Word formation

8 Circle the correct words.

1 My parents are the happiest marry / marriage / (married) couple I know.
2 I have great sympathise / sympathetic / (sympathy) for those who can't make friends easily.
3 Joe isn't a very communication / (communicative) / communicate person; he doesn't talk much.
4 This has got to be the most boredom / (boring) / bore film ever; I'm falling asleep!
5 I don't like to say, but I think my sister's engage / (engagement) / engaged was a mistake.
6 A good friend would never (embarrass) / embarrassment / embarrassed you in front of others.
7 Many young people find it difficult to (please) / pleasure / pleasant their parents.
8 After the argue / (argument) / argumentative, we didn't speak for days.

9 Use the word in capitals to form a word that fits in the gap.

1 You have terrible manners! You are a(n) ___*embarrassment*___ to the whole family! **EMBARRASS**
2 My husband and I were ___*engaged*___ for five years before we finally 'tied the knot'. **ENGAGE**
3 Friendships are one of life's greatest ___*pleasures*___. **PLEASE**
4 Their ___*marriage*___ lasted for over 20 years, but they are now separated. **MARRY**
5 Whenever I need a(n) ___*sympathetic*___ ear, I go to my mum! **SYMPATHY**
6 People who constantly talk about themselves are very ___*boring*___. **BORE**
7 Why must you be so ___*argumentative*___? Can't you just agree for once? **ARGUE**
8 Many couples break up these days because of a lack of ___*communication*___. **COMMUNICATE**

Unit 7

Exam Practice

Sentence transformation

10 Complete the second sentence so that it has a similar meaning to the first sentence, using the word given. Do not change the word given. You must use between two and five words.

1. They broke up? I can't think of anything to say!
   loss
   They broke up? I'm _____*at a loss for*_____ words!

2. We know Margo is your best friend, but we really dislike her.
   stand
   We know Margo is your best friend, but we _____*can't stand*_____ her.

3. Oh, Mum! Why are you constantly making my life more difficult?
   hard
   Oh, Mum! Why are you constantly _____*giving me a hard*_____ time?

4. I know exactly what Sammy's going through; I got divorced too.
   identify
   I can _____*identify with*_____ Sammy; I got divorced too.

5. Dean really loves his Dad, but the two never agree on anything.
   eye
   Dean really loves his Dad, but the two never _____*see eye to eye*_____ on anything.

6. Sheila is so happy! She just got into university.
   top
   Sheila is on _____*top of the world*_____! She just got into university.

7. My big brother defends me all the time.
   sticks
   My big brother _____*sticks up for*_____ me all the time.

8. I am very unhappy that your room is always such a mess.
   fed
   I am _____*fed up with*_____ your room always being such a mess.

Open cloze

11 Complete the sentences with the word that best fits each gap.

1. Even though Bill and Sharon don't have much _____*in*_____ common, they like each other.
2. That's the boy _____*whose*_____ parents recently separated.
3. My Uncle Tom is wonderful; I can rely _____*on*_____ him for anything.
4. That's the shop _____*where*_____ I bought Mum's birthday present.
5. Friendships, _____*which*_____ I think are really important, require good communication.
6. Do you remember the day _____*when*_____ we first met?
7. You didn't take out the rubbish again! I can't depend _____*on*_____ you for anything!
8. My brother, _____*who*_____ works with troubled teenagers, lives in Leeds.

What Do You Think?

Speaking

12 Talk to your partner about:
- the place where your parents met.
- a day you'll always remember.
- the characteristics of your best friend / favourite family member.
- the characteristics of your pet / a friend's pet.

Unit 8

Awareness

1 Which of these sentences are correct (C) and incorrect (I)?

1. When she gets home she'll play with you. — I
2. I'll do the washing up before I go to bed. — C
3. He'll email you after he will get to the hotel. — I
4. You can't have any ice cream until you've eaten your dinner. — C
5. Once Grandma and Grandpa arrived, we'll go into the garden. — I
6. By the time your brother finishes his homework, it'll be time for bed. — C
7. Before they came, they'll call. — I
8. Will you help me with these boxes after you have eaten? — C
9. I'll fix your bike once I've fixed mine. — C
10. The documentary will be over by the time you'll get here. — I

How many did you get right? ☐

Grammar
Temporals

When we use temporals such as *when*, *before*, *after*, *until*, *once*, *by the time*, etc to talk about the future, we follow them with a present or a present perfect tense. We do not use them with a future tense.
After we **finish** our project, we'll help you with your homework.
By the time Kevin **gets** home, the food will be cold.

We use a present perfect tense to emphasise that the first action is finished before the other one starts. We cannot use a present tense if one action has finished.
You can go out and play **when** you**'ve tidied** your room. (You'll tidy your room first and then you'll go out and play.)
Once everyone **has taken** a seat, we'll get started. (Everyone will take a seat first and then we'll start.)

Grammar Exercises

2 Circle the correct words.

1. I won't give up after / **until** I've fixed this car!
2. **As soon as** / By the time Joe arrives in London, he'll visit Big Ben.
3. We'll have a big get-together until / **after** he has graduated.
4. They'll cut the grass **after** / by the time it stops raining.
5. Dean will call us until / **when** he gets home.
6. I'll read you a story as soon as / **until** you fall to sleep.
7. Will you buy a new phone **as soon as** / by the time you've saved enough money?
8. You can't use the computer the moment / **before** you've studied for the test.

Unit 8

3 **Rewrite the sentences adding commas where necessary. Put a (✓) below those which do not need a comma.**

1. My sister will look after you until your parents get home.
   ✓

2. By the time you reach the cinema we'll be there.
   By the time you reach the cinema, we'll be there.

3. The moment I find a phone I'll give you a ring.
   The moment I find a phone, I'll give you a ring.

4. We'll visit our grandparents when we go to Surrey.
   ✓

5. Before you leave I'll make you a few sandwiches.
   Before you leave, I'll make you a few sandwiches.

6. I'll buy you a treat after we've finished doing the shopping.
   ✓

7. As soon as I know what we're doing I'll text him.
   As soon as I know what we're doing, I'll text him.

8. He'll ask her to marry him after he's found a good job.
   ✓

9. They'll buy a new house once they've saved some money.
   ✓

10. Once your parents leave we'll decorate the house for the party.
    Once your parents leave, we'll decorate the house for the party.

4 **Underline the action which is finished before the other starts.**

1. You can watch a DVD when <u>you've taken out the rubbish</u>.
2. <u>Once I've watered the flowers</u>, I'll cut the grass.
3. We'll leave for the cinema as soon as <u>Megan has arrived</u>.
4. You can't have a biscuit until <u>you've eaten everything on your plate</u>.
5. The concert will begin once <u>they've dimmed the lights</u>.
6. When <u>Susan and Tom have done the washing-up</u>, they can go out.
7. She can't come and visit until <u>she's bought a car</u>.
8. After <u>he's washed the car</u>, he can play basketball with his friends.

5 **Complete the sentences with before, by the time, until, or as soon as. Use each temporal twice.**

1. _By the time_ Janet gets to her office, the flowers will be there.
2. _Before_ he surfs the Internet, he'll turn on the computer.
3. _As soon as_ I get home, I'll walk the dog.
4. He'll buy a new stereo _as soon as_ he gets a rise.
5. The food will be all gone _by the time_ your father gets home from work.
6. You can watch TV _until_ it's time for lunch.
7. I'll turn off all the lights _before_ I leave the house.
8. _Until_ you get another bike, I'll drive you to school.

6 Circle the correct temporal and complete the sentences with the correct form of the Present Simple or Future Simple (will) of the verbs in brackets.

1. I'll send you a letter before /(the moment) I _____arrive_____ (arrive) in France.
2. You can visit me (when)/ by the time I _____buy_____ (buy) my own flat.
3. We _____'ll go_____ (go) for a walk before /(after) it has stopped raining.
4. (Once)/ Before she _____reads_____ (read) the directions, she'll know how to make the cake.
5. I can't do the ironing by the time /(until) I _____wash_____ (wash) the clothes!
6. They _____won't get_____ (not get) engaged (until)/ once they both finish their studies.
7. The students won't know the results by the time /(until) they _____are_____ (be) posted on the notice board.
8. (As soon as)/ Before I get in the house, I _____'ll change_____ (change) into something cooler.

7 Complete the sentences with the correct form of the Present Simple or Future Simple (will) of the verbs in brackets.

1. The doctor _____will contact_____ (contact) you as soon as he _____has_____ (have) your results.
2. The moment the train _____gets_____ (get) into the station, I _____'ll board_____ (board) it.
3. They _____won't move_____ (not move) house until their children _____finish_____ (finish) school.
4. Once John _____returns_____ (return), we _____'ll decide_____ (decide) what to order for dinner.
5. The moment we _____open_____ (open) the gate, the dog _____will jump_____ (jump) on us!
6. When you _____complete_____ (complete) the form, I _____'ll come_____ (come) and collect it.
7. Mum and Dad _____will miss_____ (miss) me after I _____leave_____ (leave) for university.
8. He _____'ll tell_____ (tell) Brett about the party the moment he _____sees_____ (see) him.
9. I _____'ll give_____ (give) you the paper as soon as I _____take_____ (take) a look at the entertainment section.
10. She _____'ll go_____ (go) to bed after she _____reads_____ (read) one more chapter.

Vocabulary

Phrasal verbs

8 Complete the phrasal verbs using these words. You will need to use some words more than once.

apart back down on out up

1. stick _____up_____ for someone
2. look _____up_____ to someone
3. get _____on_____
4. hold _____back_____
5. let someone _____down_____
6. hang _____out_____
7. put someone _____down_____
8. make _____up_____
9. grow _____apart_____
10. ask someone _____out_____

Unit 8

9 Complete the sentences with the correct form of the phrasal verbs from 8.
1. You shouldn't ___hold back___ your emotions; it isn't good for you.
2. He wants to ___ask___ Julia ___out___, but he's scared she'll say no.
3. After Billy moved to Europe, he and his best friend slowly ___grew apart___.
4. I ___look up to___ my father because he's reliable, honest and very smart.
5. I know everyone thinks she's a great person, but she and I just don't ___get on___.
6. Those people were calling me names! Why didn't you ___stick up___ for me?
7. I spend a lot of time in the park ___hanging out___ with my friends.
8. After the argument, it took Joe and Fran a long time to ___make up___ with each other.
9. Why are you constantly ___putting___ me ___down___? You have to stop making me feel stupid all the time.
10. I'm so sorry I ___let___ you and Dad ___down___, Mum. It'll never happen again!

Exam Practice

Word formation

10 Use the word in capitals to form a word that fits in the gap.
1. There's something wrong with Mum; she's sad and ___irritated___ all the time. **IRRITATE**
2. The man who entered the burning building is the most ___courageous___ person I know. **COURAGE**
3. People who risk their lives on the job often have to make lots of ___personal___ sacrifices. **PERSON**
4. It takes a lot of effort to make ___relationships___ work. **RELATION**
5. I've got lots of casual ___acquaintances___, but only very few close friends. **ACQUAINT**
6. ___Strangers___ are just friends you haven't met yet! **STRANGE**
7. Once you get to know people at your new school, it'll be plain ___sailing___. **SAIL**
8. You've been a great friend and I'm ___appreciative___ of all you've done for me. **APPRECIATE**

Open cloze

11 Complete the sentences with the word that best fits each gap.
1. Helen Keller devoted much of her life ___to___ helping others.
2. He's very thankful ___for___ all the advice you gave him.
3. These people are here to assist you ___with/in___ your research.
4. ___As___ soon as I get some money, I'll send her some flowers.
5. We'll call you ___the___ moment we reach the hotel.
6. I'll wait ___until___ you've finished eating and then come over.
7. You can't go out until you ___have___ made your bed.
8. ___When___ they go to Germany, they'll go to a football match in Berlin.

What Do You Think?

Writing

12 Read the writing task below and write a short story in your notebook. Try to start with a dramatic opening sentence and add a twist to your story to add suspense. Use descriptive adjectives and adverbs, idiomatic expressions and direct speech to make your story more interesting for the reader.

Begin your short story with the sentence:
Why didn't my best friend, Nellie, want to hang out with me anymore?

Review 2

Grammar

1 Circle the correct words.

1 Countless numbers of plant and animal species (have become) / have been becoming extinct in the last 20 years or so.
2 Over the decades, deforestation caused / (has caused) a great loss of natural habitat in parts of the rainforest.
3 The zoologist (returned) / has returned from her research centre in Borneo a week ago.
4 I have been / (was) lucky enough to see a herd of elephants when I visited Africa.
5 A team of experts studied / (has been studying) the effects of global warming for years now.
6 The politician has passed / (passed) a law to ban illegal hunting in 2004.
7 The use of renewable energy (has lessened) / lessened our dependence on fossil fuels in the past few years.
8 What (has your son been doing) / did your son do since he graduated from Oxford?

2 Complete the sentences with a, an, the or (–).

1 We must do something to help __the__ environment before it's too late.
2 Can you understand why __–__ people don't do something about poaching?
3 My doctor advised me to eat something light for __–__ lunch each day.
4 Aunt Edna is __an__ archaeologist; she's been to some interesting places.
5 There is an orangutan in the tree. __The__ orangutan is best friends with a dog!
6 Do you know where __the__ Galápagos Islands are located?
7 My uncle has travelled the world and speaks many languages; he even speaks __–__ Swahili!
8 My dad said he would take us skiing in __the__ Alps; I'm on top of the world!
9 Have you ever seen __the__ dolphin in the wild?
10 I don't like trains; let's go by __a__ plane instead.

3 Choose the correct answers.

1 In the USA, turning 16 is a time ___ girls have Sweet Sixteen parties.
   a that
   (b) when
2 My cousin, ___ mother is an ecologist, really cares about the planet.
   (a) whose
   b who his
3 That's the building ___ they're doing research on the effects of global warming.
   (a) where
   b which
4 This is the café ___ my husband asked me to marry him.
   a that
   (b) where
5 My father, ___ I really look up to, is a great person.
   (a) who
   b that
6 The cat ___ comes into our garden all the time kills birds.
   (a) that
   b who
7 In the autumn, ___ the leaves change colour, we like to go for drives in the countryside.
   a who
   (b) when
8 The documentary, ___ is about deforestation, starts at nine o'clock.
   a that
   (b) which

Review 2

4 Find the mistake (A or B), then write the correct sentence underneath.

1. By the time you'll (A) get home, breakfast will be (B) cooked.
   By the time you get home, breakfast will be cooked. — A

2. Before she visits (A) the Greek island, she books (B) her room.
   Before she visits the Greek island, she will book her room. — B

3. When I'll complete (A) my project, I'll go (B) out with my friends.
   When I complete/have completed my project, I will go out with my friends. — A

4. Susie moves (A) to Zambia when she gets (B) her university degree.
   Susie will move to Zambia when she gets her university degree. — A

5. After I've finished (A) writing out the invitations, I send (B) them.
   After I've finished writing out the invitations, I'll send them. — B

6. They watched (A) TV as soon as they've had (B) lunch.
   They'll watch TV as soon as they've had lunch. — A

7. Don't worry. He'll email (A) you the moment he'll arrive (B) in Brazil.
   Don't worry. He'll email you the moment he arrives / has arrived in Brazil. — B

8. Kevin will play (A) computer games until he has done (B) the washing-up.
   Kevin won't play computer games until he has done the washing-up. — A

9. Nancy will buy (A) a present before she went (B) to the party.
   Nancy will buy a present before she goes to the party. — B

10. My parents will buy (A) a smaller house after my brother and I'll leave (B) home.
    My parents will buy a smaller house after my brother and I leave / have left home. — B

5 Find the mistakes and correct the sentences.

1. The Dodo bird was extinct for over 300 years now.
   The Dodo bird has been extinct for over 300 years now.

2. I always turn out the lights after I leave the house.
   I always turn out the lights before I leave the house.

3. Tina is only 20, but she's gone to Europe, Asia and South America!
   Tina is only twenty but she's been to Europe, Asia and South America!

4. My best friend, that is an amazing student, always helps me with maths.
   My best friend, who is an amazing student, always helps me with maths.

5. Those scientists have travelled to the Easter Island.
   Those scientists have travelled to Easter Island.

6. We'll never forget the time which we saw an adult ape.
   We'll never forget the time when we saw an adult ape.

7. Billy has been to the conference; he'll be back tomorrow.
   Billy has gone to the conference; he'll be back tomorrow.

8. That crazy dog has dug in the garden for hours!
   That crazy dog has been digging in the garden for hours!

9. They won't start the match until the rain will stop.
   They won't start the match until the rain stops.

10. I've been waiting for a hour now; where are you?
    I've been waiting for an hour now; where are you?

6 Circle the correct words.

1 We've been studying botany since / **for** two weeks.
2 Can your brother play **the** / an harmonica?
3 The platypus, that / **which** is a strange creature, lives in Australia.
4 Loggers have been **cutting** / cut down trees in the rainforest for years.
5 When I grow up, I **will help** / have helped the planet.
6 Dr James has discovered / **discovered** a new species of lizard in May.
7 I'm going to – / **the** school on Elm Street to play football.
8 My mother, **who** / whose teaches English, speaks French too.
9 Julia has been / **has gone** to the library; she'll be right back.
10 You can't have dessert as soon as / **until** you've eaten your vegetables.

Use of English
Open cloze

7 Complete the sentences with the word that best fits each gap.

1 When we get to the centre, we ____*will*____ give you a call.
2 The explorer has been in Antarctica ____*since*____ 2003.
3 I was so surprised at the news that I was at ____*a*____ loss for words.
4 My parents and I have ____*been*____ to many countries in Europe.
5 I can't come out; I haven't finished my homework ____*yet*____.
6 I refuse to give up ____*until*____ I find a solution!
7 Our professor is ____*the*____ best in his field; we all look up to him.
8 Have you ____*ever*____ met anyone famous?
9 ____*How*____ long has your brother been studying butterflies?
10 Friends sometimes grow ____*apart*____ as they get older.

Word formation

8 Use the word in capitals to form a word that fits in the gap.

1 You did a good job training your dog; it's really ____*obedient*____. **OBEY**
2 I'm sometimes ____*irritated*____ by the fact that people don't seem to care. **IRRITATE**
3 My mother wants to thank you for your support; she's very ____*appreciative*____. **APPRECIATE**
4 Why don't you talk about your feelings? You should be more ____*communicative*____. **COMMUNICATE**
5 The police became ____*suspicious*____ when they saw that the man had a gun. **SUSPECT**
6 Eating fruit and vegetables is ____*beneficial*____ for your health. **BENEFIT**
7 He saved the little girl from the fire! He's so ____*courageous*____. **COURAGE**
8 Does Paul ever agree with anyone? What a(n) ____*argumentative*____ person! **ARGUE**

Review 2

Grammar

For questions 1–10, choose the word or phrase that best completes the sentence.

1. Is that the place ___ the penguins live?
   A when
   B which
   C *where*

2. Have you been a *Greenpeace* volunteer ___ a long time?
   A since
   B *for*
   C yet

3. People used to believe that ___ sun went around the earth.
   A an
   B a
   C *the*

4. They ___ on an expedition to the rainforest last year.
   A *went*
   B have been
   C have gone

5. ___ Dad gets home, he'll fix your bike.
   A *When*
   B Until
   C Before

6. We ___ around in this cave for hours!
   A walked
   B have walked
   C *have been walking*

7. Brett, ___ lives in the house next to mine, is my best friend.
   A *who*
   B that
   C whose

8. As soon as I get to the office, I ___ the professor.
   A have emailed
   B *will email*
   C emailed

9. Botany, ___ is a subject I love, is very interesting.
   A that
   B *which*
   C who

10. My grandmother is in ___ hospital. I hope she gets out soon.
    A *–*
    B an
    C the

Vocabulary

For questions 11–20 choose the word or phrase that best completes the sentence.

11. The protest is meant to ___ attention to whale hunting.
    A get
    B pay
    C bring

12. Why are you always putting Shelley ___? I thought she was our friend.
    A *down*
    B away
    C apart

13. Don't people care that so many animals are ___ the verge of extinction?
    A at
    B in
    C *on*

14. We have great ___ for the poor and the homeless.
    A sympathise
    B *sympathy*
    C sympathetic

15. He's my baby brother! Of course I stick ___ for him!
    A at
    B in
    C *up*

16. Cycling instead of driving is a good way to ___ pollution.
    A *fight*
    B save
    C take

17. ___ years of marriage, the couple have decided to separate.
    A Across
    B *After*
    C Before

18. Young people need to help raise awareness ___ the world's problems.
    A around
    B upon
    C *about*

19. ___ is something many elderly people have to deal with.
    A *Boredom*
    B Bore
    C Boring

20. This shop sells everything ___ shoes to shovels!
    A for
    B *from*
    C with

52

Unit 9

Awareness

1 Which of these sentences are correct (C) and incorrect (I)?

1. I'm cold. I'm going to put on a jacket. _I_
2. They're going to move house at the weekend. _C_
3. My boyfriend will be a famous rapper some day! _C_
4. Sally isn't going to do that again. She promised. _I_
5. Stop making noise or I'll tell your father! _C_
6. My grandmother is going to be 70 years old next Wednesday. _I_
7. Maybe we'll visit the Empire State Building when we're in New York. _C_
8. Here, I'll help you move that table. _C_
9. Are you going to take the rubbish out, please? _I_
10. Look! That little boy will fall down the stairs. _I_

How many did you get right?

Grammar

Future Simple

Affirmative	Negative	Questions
I/he/she/it/we/you/they **will** clean	I/he/she/it/we/you/they **will not (won't)** clean	**Will** I/he/she/it/we/you/they clean?
Short Answers		
Yes, I/he/she/it **will**. **Yes**, we/you/they **will**.	**No**, I/he/she/it **won't**. **No**, we/you/they **won't**.	

We use the Future Simple
• for decisions made at the time of speaking.
I'll ask my father to take us to school.
• for predictions without having evidence.
My daughter will be rich someday.
• for promises.
We won't make a mess again. We promise.
• for threats.
Don't tell anyone what he said or he'll never tell you anything ever again!
• to talk about future facts.
Karen will be 12 years old next week.
• after verbs like *think, believe, be sure, expect,* etc and words like *probably, maybe,* etc.
We expect they'll share a flat when they move to the city.
• to offer to do something for someone.
Mum will help you do the washing up.
• to ask someone to do something.
Will you tidy the living room this afternoon, please?

Be Going To

Affirmative	Negative	Questions
I **am ('m) going to** clean he/she/it **is ('s) going to** clean we/you/they **are ('re) going to** clean	I **am ('m) not going to** clean he/she/it **is not (isn't) going to** clean we/you/they **are not (aren't) going to** clean	**Am** I **going to** clean? **Is** he/she/it **going to** clean? **Are** we/you/they **going to** clean?
Short Answers		
Yes, I **am**. **Yes**, we/you/they **are**. **Yes**, he/she/it **is**.	**No**, I'm **not**. **No**, we/you/they **aren't**. **No**, he/she/it **isn't**.	

Unit 9

We use *be going to* for
- future plans.

We're going to clear out the attic at the weekend.
- predictions for the near future based on present situations or evidence.

*Oh no! That paint is wet and Billy **is going to get** it all over his trousers.*

> **Note**
>
> Some common time expressions that are often used with the Future Simple and *be going to* are *this week/month/summer, tonight, this evening, tomorrow, tomorrow morning/afternoon/night, next week/month/year, at the weekend, in January, in a few minutes/hours/days, on Thursday, on Wednesday morning*, etc.
>
> *He is going to move house **next summer**.*

Grammar Exercises

2 Tick the correct use of the Future Simple.

1. We'll go to the market for you, Mum.
   - a to offer to do something for someone ✓
   - b to talk about future facts ☐
2. My children will live in castles one day!
   - a for threats ☐
   - b for predictions without having any evidence ✓
3. Will you please vacuum the rugs for me?
   - a to ask someone to do something ✓
   - b after certain verbs ☐
4. He won't make a mess in the kitchen. He promised.
   - a for decisions made at the time of speaking ☐
   - b for promises ✓
5. Don't spill that milk or I'll make you go to your room!
   - a for threats ✓
   - b for predictions without having any evidence ☐
6. I'll get my coat and meet you at the library.
   - a for decisions made at the time of speaking ✓
   - b to ask someone to do something ☐
7. The twins will be five years old next week.
   - a for promises ☐
   - b to talk about future facts ✓
8. She believes she'll find a cheap flat in the city centre.
   - a to offer to do something for someone ☐
   - b after certain verbs ✓

3 Use the prompts to write questions, then complete the short answers. Use the Future Simple.

1. he have a party on his birthday this year?
   A: Will he have a party on his birthday this year?
   B: No, he won't.

2. you eat fast food on Saturday night?
   A: Will you eat fast food on Saturday night?
   B: Yes, I will.

3. she go to university when she finishes school?
   A: Will she go to university when she finishes school?
   B: No, she won't.

4. they travel to Dubai next winter?
   A: Will they travel to Dubai next winter?
   B: No, they won't.

5. we hang out at Tom's house at the weekend?
   A: Will we hang out at Tom's house at the weekend?
   B: Yes, we will.

6. you be an architect when you grow up?
   A: Will you be an architect when you grow up?
   B: No, I won't.

7. Tom and Margaret buy a bungalow after they get married?
   A: Will Tom and Margaret buy a bungalow after they get married?
   B: Yes, they will.

8. Jake plant a garden at his cottage in the summer?
   A: Will Jake plant a garden at his cottage in the summer?
   B: Yes, he will.

4 Answer the questions for you. Use the Future Simple and I think, I believe, I am sure, I expect, I hope, I doubt and the words probably and maybe.

1. What will you have for lunch today?
   Student's own answers

2. Who will you live with when you're an adult?

3. Where will you be at five o'clock tomorrow evening?

4. When will you move out of your parents' house?

5. What kind of house will you buy when you're older?

6. Where will you go on holiday this summer?

7. When will you next visit relatives?

8. What will you get your parents for their next anniversary?

Unit 9

5 **What will the future be like? Use the prompts to write sentences. Use the Future Simple.**

1 Robots and machines / do all the work ✓
   Robots and machines will do all the work.

2 People / travel to work and school by helicopter ✗
   People won't travel to work and school by helicopter.

3 Pollution / get worse and worse ✓
   Pollution will get worse and worse.

4 Families / go on holidays to other planets ✗
   Families won't go on holidays to other planets.

5 People / live in huge skyscrapers ✓
   People will live in huge skyscrapers.

6 Children / stop learning other languages ✗
   Children won't stop learning other languages.

7 People / be healthier and have longer lives ✓
   People will be healthier and have longer lives.

8 Animals / only live in zoos ✗
   Animals won't only live in zoos.

6 **Kate and her family are going on holiday this winter. Use the prompts to write questions about their future plans, then complete the short answers.**

1 drive / to / going to / are / their destination / Kate and her family
   A: Are Kate and her family going to drive to their destination?
   B: No, they aren't.

2 on her own / going to / is / stay / Kate
   A: Is Kate going to stay on her own?
   B: No, she isn't.

3 going to / Kate and her brother / a castle / visit / are
   A: Are Kate and her brother going to visit a castle?
   B: Yes, they are.

4 Kate's brother / ski / is / going to
   A: Is Kate's brother going to ski?
   B: Yes, he is.

5 going to / are / in nice restaurants / eat / Kate and her family
   A: Are Kate and her family going to eat in nice restaurants?
   B: Yes, they are.

6 swim / are / in the sea / going to / Kate and her brother
   A: Are Kate and her brother going to swim in the sea?
   B: No, they aren't.

7 climb / going to / Kate's brother / a mountain / is
   A: Is Kate's brother going to climb a mountain?
   B: No, he isn't.

8 going to / lots of photographs / is / take / Kate
   A: Is Kate going to take lots of photographs?
   B: Yes, she is.

7 Complete the sentences with the correct form of the Future Simple of the verbs in brackets or **be going to**.

1. **A:** I've finally decided what to put in the new living room.
   B: Really? What _are you going to put_ (you / put) in there?
2. **A:** Look! It has started to rain.
   B: Oh, _will you close_ (you / close) all the windows, please?
3. **A:** Do you know your schedule for next week?
   B: Yes. We _'re going to work_ (work) on the new skyscraper in Malaysia.
4. **A:** Sammy, look what you've done!
   B: I'm sorry, Mum. I promise I _won't do_ (not do) that again.
5. **A:** Look at that dog chasing that cat!
   B: Oh no. It _'s going to hurt_ (hurt) it!
6. **A:** Have you finished decorating your new cottage yet?
   B: No, but I'm sure I _'ll finish_ (finish) very soon.
7. **A:** Did you mop the floors for me?
   B: No, we forgot but we _'ll mop_ (mop) them this afternoon.
8. **A:** How old is your brother?
   B: Tom _will turn_ (turn) 16 next Sunday.
9. **A:** Those little boys are too close to that cliff!
   B: Yes, they _'re going to fall_ (fall) off the edge!

Vocabulary

Prepositions

8 Complete the phrases with these prepositions. You will need to use some prepositions more than once.

| about   after   at   for   in   of   to   within |

1. be prepared _for_ something
2. be a statement _about_ something
3. _for_ a reason
4. compare somebody/something _to_ somebody/something else
5. take a look _at_ somebody/something
6. not be the case _at_ all
7. something _of_ the house
8. _after_ a few minutes of doing something
9. be a good case _in_ point
10. _within_ reason

9 Complete the sentences with the correct form of the prepositions from 8.

1. People should insure their homes – a good case _in_ point are the Smiths who lost everything in a fire last year.
2. They moved house _for_ a reason; their neighbours were very noisy.
3. I'll buy you any house you want _within_ reason of course; I can't afford a castle!
4. If you compare a bungalow _to_ a skyscraper, a bungalow is much smaller.
5. Take a look _at_ that cottage. Isn't it lovely?
6. When you enter the upside down house, be prepared _for_ an unusual experience!
7. Kevin isn't tired; that's not the case _at_ all. He's just lazy.
8. The windows _of_ the house were all broken during the storm.
9. This sculpture is meant to be a statement _about_ the homeless.
10. _After_ a few minutes of being in her new flat, I felt completely at home.

Unit 9

Exam Practice

Open cloze

10 Complete the sentences with the word that best fits each gap.
1. The architect ____is____ sure he'll be able to finish the house next week.
2. Clean up your mess or Mum will ____not____ let you watch TV.
3. My uncle ____will____ take us to the home exhibition.
4. ____Are____ you going to be home later this evening?
5. They've got a plan. They're ____going____ to build the largest skyscraper in the world.
6. We aren't going ____to____ move into a flat; my husband doesn't like them.
7. Oh no. That little girl ____is____ going to fall down the stairs!
8. My brother will ____be____ 19 next month.

Cloze

11 Choose the correct answers.
1. When we go camping, it'll be your job to set up the ___.
   a) tent   b) flat   c) cottage
2. My sister's going to move into a ___ of flats in the west end.
   a) square   (b) block   c) building
3. The great thing about a ___ house is that you don't share any walls with anyone.
   a) terraced   b) semi-detached   (c) detached
4. The king lived in a huge stone ___ at the very top of a mountain.
   (a) castle   b) bungalow   c) balcony
5. When I get older, I'm going to buy a tiny little ___ in the countryside.
   (a) cottage   b) lighthouse   c) block of flats
6. Mum, you look tired; I'll ___ the carpets for you.
   a) paint   b) decorate   (c) vacuum
7. If you pass me the broom, I'll ___ the kitchen floor.
   a) dust   (b) sweep   c) mop
8. Her bungalow was surrounded by a lovely white wooden ___.
   a) wall   b) gate   (c) fence

What Do You Think?

Speaking

12 Discuss these questions with a partner:
- What kind of house will you live in when you leave your parents' house?
- Will you ask your mother and father to help you pay the rent?
- Do you believe you'll live in the city or the country?
- Have you decided how many rooms your house is going to have?
- Have you planned how you are going to decorate your house?
- Do you think you will share your new house with anyone else?

Unit 10

Awareness

1 Which of these sentences are correct (C) and incorrect (I)?

1. He won't be working in the garden all weekend.   C
2. Have they be moving into their new bungalow tomorrow?   I
3. We're visiting our relatives in the countryside next month.   C
4. Will the designer have finish the redecorating by next Tuesday?   I
5. She won't have finished painting her room by noon.   C
6. We'll be doing our shopping at this time tomorrow morning.   C
7. Next week I'll have living in this town for five years.   I
8. Bob and Sue will have planted the flowers by the end of the week.   C
9. The train will arrives at nine o'clock in the morning.   I
10. I'll have be cleaning the house all day.   I

How many did you get right? ☐

Grammar

Future Continuous

Affirmative	Negative	Questions
I/he/she/it/we/you/they **will be** clean**ing**	I/he/she/it/we/you/they **will not (won't) be** clean**ing**	**Will** I/he/she/it/we/you/they **be** clean**ing**?
Short Answers		
Yes, I/he/she/it **will.** Yes, we/you/they **will.**	No, I/he/she/it **won't.** No, we/you/they **won't.**	

Spelling: tak**e** → tak**ing**, swim → swi**mm**ing, stu**dy** → stu**dy**ing

We use the Future Continuous for
• actions that will be in progress at a specific time in the future.
*We **will be painting** the house all weekend.*
• plans and arrangements for the future.
*She **will be doing** laundry tomorrow morning.*

> **Note**
>
> Some common time expressions that are often used with the Future Continuous are *this time next week/month/summer, this time tomorrow morning/afternoon/night,* etc.
> ***This time next month** we will be moving into our new flat.*

Future Perfect Simple

Affirmative	Negative	Questions
I/he/she/it/we/you/they **will have** clean**ed**	I/he/she/it/we/you/they **will not (won't) have** clean**ed**	**Will** I/he/she/it/we/you/they **have** clean**ed**?
Short Answers		
Yes, I/he/she/it **will.** Yes, we/you/they **will.**	No, I/he/she/it **won't.** No, we/you/they **won't.**	

Spelling: talk → talk**ed**, danc**e** → danc**ed**, travel → trave**ll**ed, ti**dy** → ti**di**ed, stay → stay**ed**
We use the Future Perfect Simple to talk about

Unit 10

- something that will be finished by or before a specific time in the future.
*The builder **will have completed** the roof of the house by the end of next week.*
- the length of time that an action will have lasted for at a point of time in the future.
*Next month the architect **will have worked** on this project for six months.*

> **Note**
> Some verbs are irregular and do not follow these spelling rules. See a list of irregular verbs on pages 156-157.

> **Note**
> Some common time expressions that are often used with the Future Perfect Simple are *by the end of this week/month/year, by this time tomorrow, by tomorrow morning / ten o'clock / 2012,* etc.
> *The plumber will have fixed the problem **by twelve o'clock**.*

> **Note**
> Other tenses that describe the future are the Present Simple for timetabled events, and the Present Continuous for plans and arrangements.

Grammar Exercises

2 Tom and his family have just moved into their new home. Use the prompts to write sentences about what they will/won't be doing in the future.

1. Tom / do all the hard work ✗
   Tom won't be doing all the hard work.
2. Tom and his family / clean the house all morning ✓
   Tom and his family will be cleaning the house all morning.
3. Tom / play with his friends all day tomorrow ✗
   Tom won't be playing with his friends all day tomorrow.
4. Tom's mother / hang curtains at this time tomorrow ✓
   Tom's mother will be hanging curtains at this time tomorrow.
5. Tom's father / paint the door and window frames at this time next week ✗
   Tom's father won't be painting the door and window frames at this time next week.
6. Tom and his sister / decorate their rooms at this time tomorrow afternoon ✗
   Tom and his sister won't be decorating their rooms at this time tomorrow afternoon.
7. Tom / help his parents for the next few days ✓
   Tom will be helping his parents for the next few days.
8. Tom and his family / sleep in their new beds tonight ✓
   Tom and his family will be sleeping in their new beds tonight.

3 Use the prompts to write questions, then complete the short answers. Use the Future Continuous.

1. (he / prepare) for the birthday party all morning?
   A: Will he be preparing for the birthday party all morning?
   B: No, he won't.

2. (they / look) at new homes at nine o'clock tonight?
   A: Will they be looking at new homes at nine o'clock tonight?
   B: No, they won't.

3. (your parents / live) in their new cottage this time next summer?
   A: Will your parents be living in their new cottage this time next summer?
   B: Yes, they will.

4. (we / work) on the housing project all next month?
   A: Will we be working on the housing project all next month?
   B: Yes, we will.

5. (you / sleep) at this time tomorrow night?
   A: Will you be sleeping at this time tomorrow night?
   B: No, I won't.

6. (Pete / build) the fence in the garden on Saturday?
   A: Will Pete be building the fence in the garden on Saturday?
   B: No, he won't.

7. (you / cook) breakfast at this time tomorrow morning?
   A: Will you be cooking breakfast at this time tomorrow morning?
   B: Yes, I will.

8. (she / sell) her flat at this time next month?
   A: Will she be selling her flat at this time next month?
   B: No, she won't.

4 Use the prompts to write questions, then complete the short answers. Use the Future Perfect Simple.

1. the grass / will / have cut / by two o'clock / the gardener
   A: Will the gardener have cut the grass by two o'clock?
   B: No, he won't.

2. tomorrow evening / you / by this time / will / dinner / have had
   A: Will you have had dinner by this time tomorrow evening?
   B: No, I won't.

3. Helen / will / by next month / have completed / the house / painting
   A: Will Helen have completed painting the house by next month?
   B: Yes, she will.

4. they / paying / will / have finished / by the end of this year / for the flat
   A: Will they have finished paying for the flat by the end of this year?
   B: Yes, they will.

5. for five hours / will / by tonight / on these shelves / we / have worked
   A: Will we have worked on these shelves for five hours by tonight?
   B: Yes, we will.

6. your grandparents / in this house / for a decade / have lived / next year / will
   A: Will your grandparents have lived in this house for a decade next year?
   B: No, they won't.

7. interior design / you / for six months / have studied / by the end of this month / will
   A: Will you have studied interior design for six months by the end of this month?
   B: No, I won't.

8. have known / we / our neighbours / by the end of this week / will / for three weeks
   A: Will we have known our neighbours for three weeks by the end of this week?
   B: Yes, we will.

Unit 10

5 Complete the sentences with the correct form of the Future Perfect Simple of the verbs in brackets.

By the end of this century …
1. our lives _will have changed_ (change) in a variety of ways.
2. we _won't have found_ (not find) a solution to the problem of global warming.
3. scientists _will have discovered_ (discover) a cure for many common diseases.
4. experts _will have invented_ (invent) new technology to heat our homes.
5. _will_ people _have realised_ (realise) that we need to build homes for the poor?
6. we _'ll have started_ (start) to grow most of our food in laboratories.
7. we _won't have stopped_ (not stop) people from cutting down forests to build cities.
8. we _'ll have recognised_ (recognise) that there are too many people on the planet.

6 Tick the correct use of the future tenses.
1. Tony will have lived in the city for three months by this time next month.
   a. for something that will be finished by or before a specific time in the future ☐
   b. for the length of time that an action will have lasted for at a point of time in the future ✓
2. The upside down house closes at six o'clock in the evening.
   a. for timetabled events ✓
   b. for actions that will be in progress at a specific time in the future ☐
3. Next year the architect will have worked for this firm for five years.
   a. for the length of time that an action will have lasted for at a point of time in the future ✓
   b. for plans and arrangements for the future ☐
4. Will you have finished cleaning out the attic by next week?
   a. for actions that will be in progress at a specific time in the future ☐
   b. for something that will be finished by or before a specific time in the future ✓
5. Are you seeing the landlord later?
   a. for plans and arrangements ✓
   b. for something that will be finished by or before a specific time in the future ☐
6. Sally won't be mopping the floors at this time tomorrow morning.
   a. for actions that will be in progress at a specific time in the future ✓
   b. for the length of time that an action will have lasted for at a point of time in the future ☐
7. We'll be visiting the home exhibition all day tomorrow.
   a. for actions that will be in progress at a specific time in the future ✓
   b. for timetabled events ☐
8. Nancy and Ned will be shopping for new bedroom furniture tomorrow.
   a. for something that will be finished by or before a specific time in the future ☐
   b. for plans and arrangements for the future ✓

7 Circle the correct words.

1. **A:** What **will you be doing** / will you have done at this time tomorrow?
   B: I'm not sure yet. I'll call you.
2. **A:** What are Grant's plans?
   B: He **is flying** / will have flown to Montreal tomorrow morning.
3. **A:** Let's ask Joan to come.
   B: No, she will have cleaned / **will be cleaning** the flat all afternoon.
4. **A:** Those windows have been broken for weeks!
   B: Well, I'm afraid we **won't have fixed** / won't be fixing them by tomorrow.
5. **A:** Why are Frank and Jan so excited?
   B: Oh, they **will be moving** / will have moved into their new bungalow tomorrow.
6. **A:** You look down in the dumps, Joe. What's the matter?
   B: Well, it seems I won't have gone / **won't be going** to Paris next week after all.
7. **A:** Do you know the furniture shop's opening hours?
   B: Yes, it is opening / **opens** at 9 am and **closes** / will have closed at 5 pm.
8. **A:** By next month, Dad **will have installed** / will be installing all the new plumbing.
   B: That's good. He'll be glad to get that finished.
9. **A:** Next month they will be working / **will have worked** for the construction company for two years.
   B: Really. Has it been that long?
10. **A:** When will he have bought / **will he be buying** a new house?
    B: Next year.

Vocabulary

Collocations & Expressions

8 Complete the collocations and expressions using these words. You will need to use them more than once.

| do | make | move | take |

1. _take_ a bath
2. _take_ a break
3. _make_ a mess
4. _move_ house
5. _move_ mountains
6. _make_ payments
7. _do_ the dishes
8. _do_ the housework
9. _move_ with the times
10. _make_ your bed

9 Complete the sentences with the correct form of the expressions from 8.

1. You aren't going anywhere until you get in your room and _make_ your _bed_.
2. I'm hot and dirty from working in the garden. I need to _take a bath_; a hot one!
3. I don't mind if you cook, but make sure you don't _make a mess_ in the kitchen.
4. We didn't want to _move house_, but my wife got a really good job offer in London.
5. The only thing I hate about _doing the housework_ is vacuuming the carpets.
6. Your father has _moved mountains_ to save enough money to buy this detached house!
7. Your furniture is ancient! _Move with the times_, Carol, go buy some modern things.
8. I'll be _making payments_ on this flat until I'm 80; it'll never be paid for!
9. Vince broke his mother's favourite plate while he was _doing the dishes_.
10. We've been painting for hours; let's _take a break_.

Unit 10

Exam Practice

Open cloze

10 Complete the sentences with the word that best fits each gap.

1. My aunt and uncle are visiting and they are eating me ____*out*____ of house and home.
2. Can you believe next week we ____*will*____ have lived here for three years?
3. My father never donates money to causes; he says charity ____*begins*____ at home.
4. Tony is happy as he'll ____*be*____ selling his old cottage next week.
5. ____*By*____ tomorrow, your new curtains will be ready for you to pick up.
6. In the old days it was always the man who worked to ____*bring*____ home the bacon.
7. I've climbed ____*up*____ and down these stairs 50 times today – I'm exhausted!
8. You can ask ____*until*____ the cows come home; you're not getting your own bedroom.

Cloze

11 Choose the correct answers.

1. Is it true that the government is putting that old lighthouse on the ___?
   - **(a) market**   b shop   c stall
2. If you see my ___, can you tell him I'll be moving out of my flat at the end of the year?
   - a boss   **(b) landlord**   c architect
3. They'll have finished building the ___ onto the back of the house soon.
   - **(a) extension**   b extend   c extending
4. I'm tired of paying ___ on my flat every month; I want to buy a house.
   - a wages   **(b) rent**   c salary
5. I'm freezing; touch that ___ and see if it's hot.
   - a rug   b carpet   **(c) radiator**
6. Can you go down to the ___ and see if any water has leaked in?
   - **(a) basement**   b attic   c ceiling
7. We won't be able to come; we'll be seeing the ___ agent at this time tomorrow.
   - a central   **(b) estate**   c next-door
8. I met my new neighbour and, luckily, we ___ on like a house on fire.
   - a let   **(b) get**   c take

What Do You Think?

Writing

12 Read the writing task below and write the email.

You have received an email from your cousin, Tom, who is asking you for some advice about how to deal with some noisy neighbours. Write an email to your cousin giving him some advice about what you would do about the problem. Try to use expressions such as:

- *It's not a good idea to …*
- *I suggest that you …*
- *If I were you, I'd …*
- *Why don't you …*
- *How/What about …*

Unit 11

Awareness

1 Which of these sentences are correct (C) and incorrect (I)?

1. If you're fit and like challenges, sign up today! — C
2. Would you become a star athlete if you can? — I
3. If a player touches the ball with his hands he gets a penalty. — I
4. When the ball goes into the net, a red light comes on. — C
5. If it doesn't stop raining, they cancel the match. — I
6. If the sun will come out, we can go swimming. — I
7. He would feel better if he got up off that couch! — C
8. If I scored eight goals, I would be a hero! — C
9. If Susie were taller, she would be better at basketball. — C
10. The coach won't be happy if we do our very best. — I

How many did you get right?

Grammar

Zero Conditional

If clause	Main clause
present simple	present simple

We use the zero conditional to talk about the results of an action or situation that are always true. We can use *when* instead of *if*.
If a player **gets** the ball in the net, he **scores** a point.
When a player **gets** the ball in the net, he **scores** a point.

First Conditional

If clause	Main clause
present tense	*will* + bare infinitive

We use the first conditional to talk about the results of an action or situation that will probably happen now or in the future.
If I **win** the tournament, I**'ll be very pleased**.
If it**'s snowing** later, we**'ll go sledding**.

We can use *can*, *could*, *may* or *might* in the main clause instead of *will*. We can also use an imperative.
If Tabitha does that again, she **might get** a red card.
If the equipment isn't too heavy, **take** it out onto the pitch.

Second Conditional

If clause	Main clause
past tense	*would* + bare infinitive

We use the second conditional to talk about the results of an action or situation
• that probably won't happen now or in the future.
I **would be** more fit if I **took up** jogging.
• that we know will not happen now or in the future.
If your grandmother **won** the marathon, she**'d be** in all the papers!

We can also use the second conditional to give advice.
If I **were** you, I**'d try out** for the basketball team.

We can use *could* or *might* in the main clause instead of *would*.
Sally **could** win the race if she tried harder.
If you left now, you **might** manage to get tickets for the match.

> **Note**
> We usually use *were* for all persons in second conditional sentences.
> If Pam **were** better at soccer, she'd be in the team.

Unit 11

> **Unless**
> We can use *unless* in first and second conditional sentences. It means the same as *if not*.
> Luke won't play golf tomorrow **unless** it is a nice sunny day.
> We couldn't take part in the baseball match **unless** we had the right equipment.

Grammar Exercises

2 Use the prompts to write Zero Conditional sentences.

1. water freeze – you / put it in the freezer
   Water freezes if / when you put it in the freezer.
2. you / put the ball through the hoop – you / score a point
   If/When you put the ball through the hoop, you score a point.
3. you / boil water – it / turn into steam
   If/When you boil water, it turns into steam.
4. you / mix orange and brown – you / get yellow
   If/When you mix orange and brown, you get yellow.
5. raw meat spoil – you / leave it out for long
   Raw meat spoils if/when you leave it out for long.
6. you / sunbathe for hours – you / burn
   If/When you sunbathe for hours, you burn.
7. you / put ice in water – it / float
   If/When you put ice in water, it floats.
8. ice melt – you / put boiling water on it
   Ice melts if/when you put boiling water on it.

3 Look at the statements, then use the prompts to write sentences using the First Conditional.

1. I don't want to wear my helmet.
   (you / get hurt)
   If you don't wear your helmet, you'll get hurt.
2. Let's watch the match a little longer.
   (we / miss the bus)
   If we watch the match a little longer, we'll miss the bus.
3. I don't want to go to practice.
   (you / not improve your skills)
   If you don't go to practice, you won't improve your skills.
4. We want to go to the stadium.
   (we / see some famous footballers)
   If we go to the stadium, we'll see some famous footballers.
5. They want to take up tennis.
   (they / be fitter)
   If they take up tennis, they'll be fitter.
6. He doesn't want to warm up first.
   (he / pull a muscle)
   If he doesn't warm up first, he'll pull a muscle.
7. Let's get tickets for the football match.
   (we / not have money for food)
   If we get tickets for the football match, we won't have money for food.
8. She doesn't want to train for the race.
   (she / not win)
   If she doesn't train for the race, she won't win.

4 Match and write sentences using the First Conditional.

1. be thirsty — d
2. feel cold — c
3. not want to have sore muscles — e
4. be hungry — b
5. twist an ankle — g
6. be tired — h
7. want to win — f
8. not want to be late for the race — a

a catch the bus on time
b eat something nutritious
c put on a sweatshirt
d drink some water
e warm up before training
f try your hardest
g see a doctor
h take a short break

1. If you are thirsty, drink some water.
2. If you feel cold, put on a sweatshirt.
3. If you don't want to have sore muscles, warm up before training.
4. If you're hungry, eat something nutritious.
5. If you twist an ankle, see a doctor.
6. If you're tired, take a short break.
7. If you want to win, try your hardest.
8. If you don't want to be late for the race, catch the bus on time.

5 Rewrite the sentences using *if* or *unless*.

1. You may be kicked off the team unless you apologise for hitting the referee.
   You may be kicked off the team if you don't apologise for hitting the referee.
2. If Stella doesn't start practising, the coach won't let her play in the match.
   Unless Stella starts practising, the coach won't let her play in the match.
3. Unless you get lots of exercise, you might gain weight.
   If you don't get lots of exercise, you might gain weight.
4. They'll miss the start of the tournament unless they leave right now.
   They'll miss the start of the tournament if they don't leave right now.
5. If Ronaldo doesn't score soon, we'll take him off the pitch.
   Unless Ronaldo scores soon, we'll take him off the pitch.
6. My trainer will be angry unless I go to every practice.
   My trainer will be angry if I don't go to every practice.
7. If you don't wear your elbow pads, you can't go skateboarding.
   Unless you wear your elbow pads, you can't go skateboarding.
8. If I don't start eating properly, I could get ill.
   Unless I start eating properly, I could get ill.

Unit 11

6 Rewrite the sentences using the Second Conditional.

1. I don't have a bike, so the coach has to drive me to the championship.
   If I had a bike, the coach wouldn't have to drive me to the championship.
2. He doesn't get any exercise, so he's unfit.
   If he got some exercise, he wouldn't be unfit.
3. She's not good at scoring goals, so she doesn't get chosen for teams.
   If she were good at scoring goals, she would get chosen for teams.
4. We don't have money, so we can't buy new team uniforms.
   If we had money, we could buy new team uniforms.
5. We don't have enough players, so we might have to cancel the match.
   If we had enough players, we might not have to cancel the match.
6. The fans don't have tickets, so they can't enter the stadium.
   If the fans had tickets, they could enter the stadium.
7. My trainer doesn't have time, so I have to train on my own today.
   If my trainer had time, I wouldn't have to train on my own today.
8. They don't have a pen, so they can't get the footballer's autograph.
   If they had a pen, they could get the footballer's autograph.

7 Complete the sentences with the correct form of the verbs in brackets. Add commas where necessary.

1. **A:** Should I join the basketball team or the hockey team?
   B: If I ___*were*___ (be) you, I ___*wouldn't join*___ (not join) either!
2. **A:** If he scores one more goal, ___*will we win*___ (we / win) the competition?
   B: No. If he ___*puts*___ (put) the ball in the net, we'll still need two more goals to tie!
3. **A:** What colour ___*do you get*___ (you / get) if you ___*mix*___ (mix) red and white?
   B: Pink.
4. **A:** I'm hungry. Do we have anything to eat?
   B: Yes. If you ___*open*___ (open) the cupboard door, you ___*will see*___ (see) lots of food.
5. **A:** We're going to be late for the match!
   B: Calm down. If we get Dad to drive us, we ___*will make*___ (make) it on time.
6. **A:** What ___*would you do*___ (you / do) if you won an Olympic medal?
   B: I ___*would jump*___ (jump) for joy!
7. **A:** I'm dying of thirst.
   B: If you ___*are*___ (be) thirsty, ___*drink*___ (drink) something!
8. **A:** I'm overweight.
   B: You ___*would be*___ (be) fitter if you ___*weren't*___ (not be) such a couch potato.
9. **A:** Why does Harriet look so stressed?
   B: Because unless she ___*hurries*___ (hurry), she ___*will miss*___ (miss) the bus.
10. **A:** Dean ___*gets*___ (get) really angry when he loses.
    B: If he ___*practised*___ (practise) more, he might not lose so often!

Vocabulary

Phrasal verbs

8 Choose the correct answers.

1. To *call off* means — **a**
   a to cancel
   b to contact
2. To *kick off* means — **a**
   a to start
   b to move
3. To *wear out* means — **b**
   a to get dressed up
   b to get old and damaged
4. To *warm up* means — **b**
   a to put on heavy clothes
   b to prepare your body
5. To *cool off* means — **a**
   a to calm down
   b to be unfashionable
6. To *cheer* someone *on* means — **b**
   a to make them happy
   b to encourage them loudly
7. To *go down as* means — **a**
   a to be remembered as
   b to take a bad fall
8. To *end up* means — **a**
   a to finish
   b to trip

9 Complete the sentences with the correct form of the phrasal verbs from 8.

1. Our team may very well ___*go down as*___ one of the worst volleyball teams in history!
2. If we win this final match, we'll ___*end up*___ in third place in the tournament.
3. I think the archery competition ___*kicks off*___ at four o'clock, so don't be late.
4. Steve usually ___*warms up*___ for about 20 minutes before he goes jogging.
5. Can you explain to me how you manage to ___*wear out*___ your trainers so quickly?
6. ___*Calm down*___! Why are you so angry? It's just a game!
7. Athletes appreciate it when fans come out to ___*cheer*___ them ___*on*___.
8. If it continues to rain, they'll have to ___*call off*___ the marathon.

Exam Practice

Cloze

10 Choose the correct answers.

1. The ___ sentenced the man to two years in prison for selling tickets illegally.
   (a) judge   b linesman   c referee
2. If he makes it around the race ___ more than once, I'll be shocked!
   a pool   b pitch   **(c) track**
3. You can't play tennis unless you've got a ___.
   a stick   **(b) racket**   c bat
4. It was a good thing Tony was wearing his ___ when he fell or he could have got a nasty head injury.
   a cap   **(b) helmet**   c glove
5. If I had a yacht, I would go ___ every day!
   a canoeing   b windsurfing   **(c) sailing**
6. You are a really good artist; you should enter the drawing ___.
   (a) competition   b championship   c final
7. We're not really keen on ___ sports like basketball; we prefer sports where we play one-on-one.
   a indoor   b individual   **(c) team**
8. The weather outside is terrible. Let's play a ___ of cards.
   (a) game   b match   c tournament

Unit 11 **69**

Unit 11

Sentence transformation

11 Complete the second sentence so that it has a similar meaning to the first sentence, using the word given. Do not change the word given. You must use between two and five words.

1. That glass of cold water was very satisfying – I was thirsty.
   hit
   That glass of cold water _____ hit the spot _____ – I was thirsty.

2. Stella's coach told her that she wasn't fast enough to enter the race; she was really upset.
   took
   Stella's coach told her that she wasn't fast enough to enter the race; that _____ took the wind out of _____ her sails.

3. If we want to save the whales, we have to take action now – it's almost too late.
   against
   If we want to save the whales, we have to take action now – it's _____ a race against _____ time.

4. The runners were right beside each other as they entered the last lap of the race.
   neck
   The runners were _____ neck and neck _____ as they entered the last lap of the race.

5. Put down that cake! If you want to lose weight, you have to begin now!
   get
   Put down that cake! If you want to lose weight, you have to _____ get the ball _____ rolling!

6. If they accuse the athletes of taking illegal drugs, it'll create a lot of problems.
   open
   If they accuse the athletes of taking illegal drugs, it'll _____ open up a can of _____ worms.

7. Your muscles will hurt a bit after your first visit to the gym, but that's to be expected.
   for
   Your muscles will hurt a bit after your first visit to the gym, but that's _____ par for the _____ course.

8. I'm not calling Shelley, she insulted me – it's up to her to do something.
   ball
   I'm not calling Shelley, she insulted me – the _____ ball is in her _____ court.

What Do You Think?

Speaking

12 Discuss these questions with a partner:
- What happens if you don't eat properly?
- What will happen if you don't exercise?
- What would you do if you were unfit?
- What would you do if the coach asked you to join a team?
- What would you do if you were a famous athlete?

Unit 12

Awareness

1 Which of these sentences are correct (C) and incorrect (I)?

1. We could have bought tickets if we wouldn't have spent all our money. _I_
2. If they had been invited to play, would they have done it? _C_
3. Terry wishes he might make the team. _I_
4. If only there was a place to go windsurfing in the area. _C_
5. She wishes she would be as fit as her sister. _I_
6. Would you wish you had trained harder for the competition? _I_
7. If I arrived at the track earlier, the coach might have let me race. _I_
8. If he had had a racket, he would have entered the tournament. _C_
9. I wish the fans wouldn't shout at me every time I make a mistake. _C_
10. Dad wishes he hadn't quit the cycling team when he was in university. _C_

How many did you get right? ☐

Grammar

Third Conditional

If clause	Main clause
past perfect tense	*would* + *have* + past participle

We use the third conditional to talk about events or situations in the past that could have happened, but didn't. These are always hypothetical things because we cannot change the past.
If they **had won** the competition, they **would have received** the gold medal. (They didn't win the competition, so they didn't receive the gold medal.)

We can use *could* or *might* in the main clause instead of *would*.
We **could have defeated** the other team if we had trained more often.
If the skateboard had been better quality, Juan **might have bought** it.

Wish & If Only

We use *wish* to talk about a situation or an action we aren't happy about, or to say how we would like something to be different.

We use *wish* + a past tense when we talk about the present or the future.
She **wishes** she **were** tall enough to play in the basketball team.

We use *wish* + a past perfect tense when we talk about the past.
We **wish** we **had looked after** our health better when we were young.

We use *wish* + *would* + bare infinitive when we talk about other people's annoying habits or to say that we would like something to be different in the future. We use it for actions, not states. We can only use *wish* + *would* when the subjects are different.
I **wish** my brother **would stop** taking my helmet without asking me first.
Taylor **wishes** he **could take part** in the card game.

We can use *If only* instead of *wish* in affirmative and negative sentences.
If only there was a swimming pool in our school.
If only I wasn't so slow. I can't join the running team.

Unit 12

Grammar Exercises

2 Match to form sentences in the Third Conditional.

1. He wouldn't have missed the chance to go canoeing — **d**
2. If she hadn't felt tired this morning, — **b**
3. If she hadn't been such a poor sport, — **e**
4. If the game hadn't been so boring, — **h**
5. They might have won the whole tournament — **c**
6. I might have taken the coaching job — **g**
7. If it hadn't been my parents' anniversary, — **a**
8. If the gloves hadn't been so expensive, — **f**

a. I could have gone golfing with my friends.
b. she would have gone to her training session.
c. if they had made it to the finals.
d. if he hadn't missed the train.
e. the others on her team would have liked her more.
f. would you have bought them?
g. if the salary had been better.
h. we would have stayed to see the end of it.

3 Complete the sentences with the correct form of the verbs in brackets using the Third Conditional.

1. If he ___hadn't been___ (not be) in such a rush, he ___would / might not have left___ (not leave) his hockey stick at home.
2. She ___would/might/could have bought___ (buy) tickets for the game if she ___had remembered___ (remember) earlier.
3. If you ___hadn't been___ (not be) so tired, you ___could have come___ (come) sailing.
4. Helen ___would/might not have hurt___ (not hurt) her leg if she ___had worn___ (wear) knee pads.
5. They ___would have been___ (be) warmer, if they ___had taken___ (take) their tracksuits.
6. If I ___had turned up___ (turn up) for practice, my coach ___would/might not have shouted___ (not shout) at me.
7. If he ___had tried___ (try) harder, ___would/could he have won___ (he / win) the marathon?
8. If our team ___had raised___ (raise) more money, we ___would/could/might have got___ (get) nicer uniforms.

4 Use the prompts to write sentences using the Third Conditional.

1. Tony / not play so badly / coach not kick him off the team
   If Tony hadn't played so badly, the coach wouldn't have kicked him off the team.
2. I / not fall on the ice / not hurt my head
   If I hadn't fallen on the ice, I wouldn't have hurt my head.
3. Sharon and Jill / have enough money / go to the London Olympics
   If Sharon and Jill had had enough money, they would have gone to the London Olympics.
4. Karen / not eat so much / gain weight?
   If Karen hadn't eaten so much, would she have gained weight?
5. Peter / not do his best / his trainer be disappointed?
   If Peter hadn't done his best, would his trainer have been disappointed?
6. I / wear my jacket / not catch a cold
   If I had worn my jacket, I wouldn't have caught a cold.
7. We / not like sports / not join the school swimming team
   If we hadn't liked sports, we wouldn't have joined the school swimming team.
8. Mum and Dad / see me play / be very proud
   If Mum and Dad had seen me play, they would have been very proud.

5 Read the paragraph, then write sentences using the Third Conditional.

Tonya wanted to watch a baseball game, so she went to the local field. She got to the field and the coach got Tonya to play. Tonya scored a lot of runs. A talent scout noticed her. He signed her to play for a professional team. Tonya played very well for the team. Tonya's team won the national championship two years later. Tonya became a star athlete.

1 *If Tonya hadn't wanted to watch a baseball game, she wouldn't have gone to the local field.*
2 *If she hadn't gone to the local field, the coach wouldn't have got her to play.*
3 *If the coach hadn't got her to play, she wouldn't have scored a lot of runs.*
4 *If she hadn't scored a lot of runs, a talent scout wouldn't have noticed her.*
5 *If the talent scout hadn't noticed her, he wouldn't have signed her to play for a professional team.*
6 *If he hadn't signed her to play for a professional team, Tonya wouldn't have played very well for the team.*
7 *If she hadn't played very well for the team, it wouldn't have won the national championship two years later.*
8 *If her team hadn't won the national championship two years later, Tonya wouldn't have become a star athlete.*

6 Coach Young is very annoyed with his team. Use the prompts to write what the coach says about the people in the team.

1 Tony / take the game seriously
   I wish Tony would take the game seriously.
2 Julia / be on time for practice
   I wish Julia would be on time for practice.
3 Cindy and Sherry / not forget their uniforms all the time
   I wish Cindy and Sherry wouldn't forget their uniforms all the time.
4 Brett / not shout at his teammates
   I wish Brett wouldn't shout at his teammates.
5 Vera / co-operate with the other players
   I wish Vera would co-operate with the other players.
6 Sam / follow my instructions
   I wish Sam would follow my instructions.
7 John and Gina / not break the rules
   I wish John and Gina wouldn't break the rules.
8 Sheila / be a better sport
   I wish Sheila would be a better sport.

7 Complete the dialogues with the correct form of the verbs in brackets.

1 **A:** Do you know it's only two o'clock?
   B: I know! I wish we _could leave_ (leave), but we don't get off work until five.
2 **A:** Tom pulled a muscle. He wishes he _had warmed up_ (warm up) before he went jogging.
   B: Yes, if only he _had asked_ (ask) us about that. We know warming up is a must.
3 **A:** Why does Jane look so down in the dumps?
   B: Oh, she wishes she _could play_ (play) on her brother's football team.
4 **A:** What's the matter, boys?
   B: We can't take part in the race. If only we _weren't_ (not be) so unfit.
5 **A:** I wish we _could go_ (go) canoeing more often.
   B: Yes, if only there _were_ (be) a river closer to home.
6 **A:** It's still raining cats and dogs.
   B: Yes, I wish it _would stop_ (stop). I want to go golfing.
7 **A:** Have you ever seen a professional basketball game?
   B: No, I wish I _had seen_ (see) the Knicks when they played in town last year.

Unit 12

Vocabulary

Word formation

8 Complete the table.

noun	verb	adjective	adverb
(1) _definition_	define	defined	definitely
competition/competitor	compete	(2) _competitive_	competitively
(3) _assistance_/assistant	assist	assistant	–
(4) _freedom_	free	free	freely
follower	(5) _follow_	following	–
(6) _concentration_	concentrate	concentrated	–
depth	deepen	(7) _deep_	deeply
(8) _supervision_/supervisor	supervise	supervised	–
danger	(9) _endanger_	dangerous	dangerously
–	–	proper	(10) _properly_

9 Complete the sentences with the correct form of the words from the table in 8.

1 My coach always says if you're going to do something, you should always do it _properly_.
2 That man is a great yoga master; he's got thousands of _followers_ who listen to his every word.
3 You'll have to improve your level of _concentration_ if you want to take up archery.
4 Kids, do not attempt this at home! You should only do this sport under the _supervision_ of an adult.
5 I believe free-diving is one of the most _dangerous_ sports in the world – I wouldn't try it.
6 I wish I'd been a(n) _competitor_ in that race! I know I could have won!
7 What is your _definition_ of a great athlete? Mine is someone who excels at sport.
8 Is anyone mad enough to jump from a plane without the _assistance_ of a parachute?
9 Who knows what strange creatures live in the _depths_ of the ocean!
10 Don't you love the sense of _freedom_ you get when you're flying down a ski slope?

Exam Practice

Open cloze

10 Complete the sentences with the word that best fits each gap.

1 People have been _holding_ sporting competitions since the first Olympics in 776 BC.
2 I hope Tim is prepared; he'll be competing _against_ some of the best skiers in the world.
3 To succeed _in_ fishing, you need the right equipment … and a lot of patience!
4 In the 50-yard dash, you have to sprint _to_ the finishing line.
5 Joe is taking part _in_ both the triple jump and the pole-vaulting events.
6 In this sport, competitors _do_ a hop and step and then jump as far as they can.
7 Can you believe it? Sanchez just _set_ a new world record!
8 OK everyone – _on_ your marks, get set, go!

Word formation

11 Use the word in capitals to form a word that fits in the gap.

1 _Athletics_ include events like running and jumping. **ATHLETE**
2 The sign on the office door simply said, 'Gone _fishing_'. **FISH**
3 The _golfer_ was hit by a bolt of lightning; luckily he survived. **GOLF**
4 My cousin Sarah is a(n) _excellent_ basketball player; I wish I were her. **EXCEL**
5 Grant was awarded a medal for his many _achievements_ in sport. **ACHIEVE**
6 This event requires a combination of _strength_ and concentration. **STRONG**
7 Jones' greatest _weakness_ is her inability to come from behind to defeat her opponents. **WEAK**
8 So far this year, my team has had four wins and seven _losses_. **LOSE**

What Do You Think?

Writing

12 Read the writing task below and write a short essay in your notebook. Try to use linking words and phrases like in addition, moreover, although, however, firstly, finally, therefore, in conclusion, etc to connect ideas, sentences and paragraphs.

Some parents make their children take part in competitive sports and games. Is this a good thing? How might this negatively affect young people? Write an essay discussing your opinions using specific examples.

Grammar

1 Circle the correct words.

1. **A:** Oh no. It's starting to snow.
   B: You're right! Are you going to tell / **(Will you tell)** Joey to come indoors, please?
2. **A:** Look at that skier. He's out of control!
   B: He will / **(is going to)** crash into that tree!
3. **A:** Do you know your plans for next month?
   B: Yes, I will fly / **(am going to fly)** to Paris to compete in a tennis tournament.
4. **A:** How old is your sister?
   B: She is going to be / **(will be)** 12 next Friday.
5. **A:** Why did you and your friends make a mess in the house?
   B: I'm sorry, Dad. I promise I am not going to do / **(won't do)** it again.
6. **A:** Have they finished installing your central heating yet?
   B: No. But I'm sure they **(will finish)** / are going to finish very soon.
7. **A:** What's your parents' schedule like for next week?
   B: They will travel / **(are going to travel)** to Asia, but they **(aren't going to stay)** / won't stay for long.
8. **A:** I've decided to take up a sport.
   B: Really? What sport **(are you going to take up)** / will you take up?

2 Complete the dialogues with the correct form of the Present Simple, Future Continuous or Future Perfect Simple of the verbs in brackets.

1. **A:** You look upset, Sally. Are you OK?
   B: Not really. It seems I _won't be playing_ (not play) in next month's hockey tournament after all.
2. **A:** What _will she be doing_ (she / do) at this time tomorrow evening?
   B: I have no idea, but if I see her, I'll get her to text you.
3. **A:** Next month Steven _will have been_ (be) my personal trainer for six months.
   B: I know. I remember the day you hired him.
4. **A:** When _will the team be getting_ (the team / get) new equipment?
   B: Next winter if we're lucky.
5. **A:** Will your coach be at the match next week?
   B: Let's look at his schedule. No. He _'ll be going_ (go) to Boston for a sports conference.
6. **A:** Is Tim coming to the tennis court?
   B: No, he _'ll be working_ (work) in his garden all afternoon.
7. **A:** By next Saturday, they _'ll have completed_ (complete) the track at the sports centre.
   B: Brilliant! I can hardly wait to train there.
8. **A:** We've been waiting for the uniforms for weeks!
   B: I'm sorry, but we _won't have sewn_ (not sew) all the names on them by tomorrow.
9. **A:** Why are Kent and Carol so busy these days?
   B: Because they _'ll be moving_ (move) into their new bungalow this time next week.
10. **A:** Do you know the opening hours of the gym?
    B: Yes, it _opens_ (open) at 8 am and _closes_ (close) at 11 pm.

3 Choose the correct answers.

1 I'll never finish the housework on time __ you help me.
   a) unless
   b) if

2 Janet __ so overweight if she got more exercise.
   a) wouldn't be
   b) won't be

3 You know, Pam, if I __ you, I wouldn't buy that house; it's too expensive.
   a) am
   b) were

4 Water __ if temperatures drop below zero degrees.
   a) will freeze
   b) freezes

5 If you aren't busy later, __ and I'll cook you dinner.
   a) would come over
   b) come over

6 If you open that window, you __ that it's much cooler.
   a) will see
   b) would see

7 If you hurry, you __ to the sports centre on time for the match.
   a) get
   b) will get

8 If they __ harder, they might do better in competitions.
   a) tried
   b) would try

9 What __ if he won a lot of money?
   a) will Tom do
   b) would Tom do

10 If we finish work early, __ to the cottage?
   a) will we go
   b) would we go

4 Complete the sentences with the word that best fits each gap.

1 I wish I ___could___ afford to move into a bigger house.
2 Stan wishes he ___had___ asked his parents for advice before he made his decision.
3 If ___only___ Nancy had won the tennis match; she would have been so pleased.
4 If I had known you were sleeping, I would ___not___ have knocked on the door.
5 If only there ___were___ more good players on my team!
6 I wish it ___would___ get colder; I want to go skiing!
7 Would you ___have___ joined the team if the coach had asked you to?
8 I wish the neighbours ___would___ stop playing football in our back garden.

5 Circle the correct answers.

1 By next week, he will be deciding / (will have decided) if he wants to join the team.
2 I wish my brother stopped / (would stop) bragging about how strong he is!
3 The fans will be thrilled if we will score / (score) one more goal.
4 Unless you stop shouting at the fans, the referee is going to give / (will give) you a yellow card.
5 They (will be going) / will be gone onto the pitch soon.
6 Susie wishes she (had) / had had a better bicycle; hers is very old.
7 Next winter I (will have worked) / will be working as an umpire for three years.
8 The ice on the river is very thin. Those skaters will / (are going to) fall through it!
9 If the player (hadn't missed) / wouldn't miss the net, his team would have won the match.
10 If only we (had bought) / bought tickets last week; now there are none left.

Review 3

Review 3

6 Find the mistakes and correct the sentences where necessary. Put a tick (✓) below those which do not need correcting.

1 The builders will be completing the tennis court by next month.
   The builders will have completed the tennis court by next month.

2 If Mum is mopping the floors this morning, she won't be able to make my birthday cake.
   ✓

3 Don't worry, Coach Myers. I'm sure we are going to get into the finals.
   Don't worry, Coach Myers. I'm sure we'll get into the finals.

4 I don't know where Timmy is. If only he tells me where he was going before he left the house!
   I don't know where Timmy is. If only he had told me where he was going before he left the house!

5 If he had known you were looking for a flat, he would give you the number of his estate agent.
   If he had known you were looking for a flat, he would have given you the number of his estate agent.

6 Next winter I'll be living in this terraced house for five years.
   Next winter I'll have lived in this terraced house for five years.

7 My parents have decided they are going to sell their house and move to the country.
   ✓

8 If you heat water, it boils.
   ✓

9 Look at those black clouds. It'll rain.
   Look at those black clouds. It's going to rain.

10 If we go jogging every day, we would lose lots of weight – but of course that will never happen!
   If we went jogging every day, we would lose lots of weight – but of course that will never happen!

Use of English
Word formation

7 Use the word in capitals to form a word that fits in the gap.

1 This house is very cold. If only the _____radiators_____ gave off more heat. **RADIATE**
2 Will they have finished the _____extension_____ on your house by next week? **EXTEND**
3 You need to improve your level of _____concentration_____ or you'll never be a top athlete. **CONCENTRATE**
4 Do not go into the pool without the _____supervision_____ of a lifeguard. **SUPERVISE**
5 By the end of this summer, I'll have taken part in six swimming _____competitions_____. **COMPETE**
6 My tennis instructor says my serve is my main _____weakness_____. **WEAK**
7 If we make it to the _____championship_____, I'll be on top of the world! **CHAMPION**
8 John isn't keen on _____athletics_____; he prefers water sports. **ATHLETE**

Sentence transformation

8 Complete the second sentence so that it has a similar meaning to the first sentence, using the word given. Do not change the word given. You must use between two and five words.

1. I don't want to disappoint you, but you aren't good enough for the Olympics yet.
   sails
   I don't want to take the ___wind out of your sails___, but you aren't good enough for the Olympics yet.

2. I need to stop for a minute; I'm exhausted from running around this track.
   break
   I need to ___take a break___; I'm exhausted from running around this track.

3. The excited fans shouted loudly, offering encouragement to their favourite player.
   on
   The excited fans ___cheered on___ their favourite player.

4. My cousins came over yesterday and they ate everything in the house.
   out
   My cousins ___ate me out of house___ and home when they came over yesterday.

5. You can exercise forever, but if you don't cut down on sweets you won't lose weight.
   cows
   You can exercise ___until the cows come home___, but if you don't cut down on sweets, you won't lose weight.

6. My trainer and I are best friends.
   house
   My trainer and I ___get on like a house___ on fire.

7. I'd like to come out, but I'll be cleaning the house all afternoon.
   doing
   I'd like to come out, but I'll be ___doing the housework___ all afternoon.

8. My uncle earns the money while my aunt stays home and looks after the baby.
   bacon
   My uncle ___brings home the bacon___ while my aunt stays home and looks after the baby.

9. You and your brother can make a cake if you keep the kitchen neat and tidy.
   mess
   If you don't ___make a mess___ in the kitchen, you and your brother can make a cake.

10. The swimmers were right beside each other as the race came to an end.
    neck
    The swimmers were ___neck and neck___ as the race came to an end.

Review 3

Review 3

Grammar

9 For questions 1–10, choose the word or phrase that best completes the sentence.

1 ___ her flat all afternoon?
  A Will she be cleaning
  B Will she have cleaning
  C Will she have cleaned

2 If only my neighbours ___ loud music every night.
  A won't play
  B haven't played
  C didn't play

3 Oh no, Ted hit the table and that vase ___!
  A is going to fall
  B will fall
  C is going fall

4 Metal rusts if you ___ it in the rain.
  A leave
  B will leave
  C are leaving

5 They ___ the kitchen if they hadn't been so busy.
  A could have painted
  B could paint
  C can paint

6 We ___ to the finals if we win this match.
  A would go on
  B will go on
  C would have gone on

7 I ___ be late for practice again, Coach Dean – I promise.
  A am not going to
  B am not going
  C won't

8 They would be happier if they ___ a detached house.
  A had
  B have
  C will have

9 This time next week we ___ in the golf tournament.
  A will play
  B will have played
  C will be playing

10 Unless you improve your serve, you ___ compete.
  A will be able to
  B won't be able to
  C would be able to

Vocabulary

10 For questions 11–20, choose the word or phrase that best completes the sentence.

11 If it keeps raining, they'll probably ___ off the game.
  A call
  B tell
  C take

12 They're at the ___; they're looking for a house to buy.
  A estate agent's
  B umpire's
  C landlord's

13 If only I didn't have to ___ all the carpets – I want to go out!
  A decorate
  B vacuum
  C paint

14 Tom is in great pain; he was hit by a cricket ___.
  A stick
  B racket
  C bat

15 It's always nice when the fans are there to ___ you on.
  A yell
  B shout
  C cheer

16 Are they really going to put that lovely old lighthouse ___ the market?
  A at
  B in
  C on

17 And the racer ___ to the finishing line; what a race!
  A sprints
  B paces
  C strolls

18 My grandfather's favourite saying was 'charity ___ at home'.
  A begins
  B ends
  C finishes

19 The home exhibition kicks ___ at 4 pm, so I'll pick you up at 3:30.
  A in
  B off
  C on

20 I'm hot and sweaty from working in the garden; I'm going to ___ a bath.
  A make
  B do
  C take

Unit 13

Awareness

1 Which of these sentences are correct (C) and incorrect (I)?

1	Sherry wasn't been scuba diving for very long.	_I_
2	I had been cycling for hours and had fainted just before reaching the town.	_I_
3	We hadn't been in the cave for long before they found us.	_C_
4	Had they been waiting since very long?	_I_
5	The competition had already begun when the storm started.	_C_
6	We had realised afterwards that we had been very lucky.	_I_
7	When the skier saw the tree, he quickly changed his course.	_C_
8	They unlocked the door and entered the house.	_C_
9	She had been struggling in the water for several minutes before her friend had been pulling her back into the boat.	_I_
10	How long had you searching for water?	_I_

How many did you get right? ☐

Grammar

Past Perfect Simple

Affirmative	Negative	Questions
I/he/she/it/we/you/they **had** (**'d**) search**ed**	I/he/she/it/we/you/they **had not** (**hadn't**) search**ed**	**Had** I/he/she/it/we/you/they search**ed**?
Short Answers		
Yes, I/he/she/it **had**. **Yes**, we/you/they **had**.	**No**, I/he/she/it **hadn't**. **No**, we/you/they **hadn't**.	

Spelling: talk → talk**ed**, dance → danc**ed**, travel → trave**lled**, tidy → ti**died**, stay → stay**ed**

We use the Past Perfect Simple for an action or situation that finished before another action, situation or time in the past.
*The lost hiker **had been** in the forest for days before rescuers found him.*

Note
Some verbs are irregular and do not follow these spelling rules. See a list of irregular verbs on pages 156–157.

Note
Some common time expressions that are often used with the Past Perfect Simple are *already, for, for a long time/ages, just, never, once, since 2007/June, so far, yet,* etc.
*The snow had **already** begun to fall when we left for the ski slope.*

Past Simple & Past Perfect Simple

In some sentences, it is clear which action happens first. In this case, we can use the Past Simple for both actions. However, when the order of events is not clear, or when we want to emphasise which action happened first, we can use the Past Perfect Simple for the first action.

They **went** to the meeting and **talked** about the expedition.
She **realised** later that she **had done** something very foolish.

Remember! We must use the Past Simple for both actions when one past action happens quickly after another or one is the immediate result of the other.
*When the little girl **heard** the loud noise, she **hid** in the wardrobe.*

Unit 13

Past Perfect Continuous

Affirmative	Negative	Questions
I/he/she/it/we/you/they had ('d) been searching	I/he/she/it/we/you/they had not (hadn't) been searching	Had I/he/she/it/we/you/they been searching?
Short Answers		
Yes, I/he/she/it had. Yes, we/you/they had.	No, I/he/she/it hadn't. No, we/you/they hadn't.	

Spelling: take → tak**ing**, swim → swim**ming**, study → study**ing**

We use the Past Perfect Continuous for
• actions that started in the past and were still in progress when another action started or when something happened.
He **had been sliding** down the hill for several minutes before he managed to grab a branch.
• actions that were in progress in the past and had an effect on a later action.
The athlete **had been running** for hours and collapsed just after crossing the finishing line.

> **Note**
>
> Some common time expressions that are often used with the Past Perfect Continuous are *all day/night/week, for years/a long time/ages, since*. We can use *How long ...?* with the Past Perfect Continuous in questions and *for (very) long* in questions and negative sentences.
>
> Stan had been going parachuting **for years**.
> **How long** had you been taking part in marathons?

Grammar Exercises

2 Complete the sentences with the correct form of the Past Perfect Simple of the verbs in brackets.

1. The skier _had returned_ (return) to the lodge before the blizzard started.
2. Shelley _had never fished_ (never / fish) in her life, but she realised she was very good at it.
3. _Had they already called_ (they / already / call) a taxi by the time you arrived?
4. Until 2008, we _had never been_ (never / be) sailing.
5. The children _hadn't tried_ (not try) out the amusement park's scariest ride yet.
6. I _had worked_ (work) as an instructor for ages and was a bit bored with my job.
7. Dean and Fran _had hiked_ (hike) in the Alps once and really enjoyed themselves.
8. _Had Kevin bought_ (Kevin / buy) snorkelling equipment before he left on his trip?

3 Todd went on an extreme holiday last month. What had he done before he left for his holiday? Use the prompts to write questions and answers in the Past Perfect Simple.

1. buy / safety equipment
   Q: What had Todd bought before he left for his holiday?
   A: He had bought safety equipment.
2. book / his flight
   Q: *What had Todd booked before he left for his holiday?*
   A: *He had booked his flight.*
3. do / online research
   Q: *What had Todd done before he left for his holiday?*
   A: *He had done online research.*
4. take / a survival course
   Q: *What had Todd taken before he left for his holiday?*
   A: *He had taken a survival course.*
5. learn / first-aid skills
   Q: *What had Todd learnt before he left for his holiday?*
   A: *He had learnt first-aid skills.*
6. ask for / time off work
   Q: *What had Todd asked for before he left for his holiday?*
   A: *He had asked for time off work.*
7. pack / his bags
   Q: *What had Todd packed before he left for his holiday?*
   A: *He had packed his bags.*
8. get / a medical check-up
   Q: *What had Todd got before he left for his holiday?*
   A: *He had got a medical check-up.*

4 Underline the action which happened first.

1. <u>After Billy had packed his rucksack</u>, he left the house.
2. <u>Gina counted to ten</u> and dived off the cliff into the water.
3. The hikers realised later that <u>they had been very close to death</u>.
4. As soon as <u>he saw the child fall in the lake</u>, the fisherman called for help.
5. When <u>we had eaten our meal</u>, we paid the bill.
6. By the time we got home, <u>Mum had washed the dishes</u>.
7. <u>I had just moved to Australia</u> when I got the chance to go snorkelling on the Great Barrier Reef.
8. The fans left the stadium because <u>the concert had finished</u>.

5 Complete the sentences with the correct form of the Past Perfect Continuous of the verbs in brackets.

1. My grandfather _had been living_ (live) in his old house for ages before he moved in with us.
2. I _had been struggling_ (struggle) with my problem for weeks before I found a solution.
3. _Had she been battling_ (she / battle) against the disease for long before she died?
4. They _hadn't been flying_ (not fly) for long when they lost radio contact.
5. How long _had you been digging_ (you / dig) before you found the buried treasure?
6. We _had been playing_ (play) in the rain since noon, so we were very wet.
7. Gillian was exhausted because she _had been walking_ (walk) in the jungle for a very long time.
8. He _hadn't been working_ (not work) at the resort for long when he decided to quit.

Unit 13

6 Circle the correct words.
1 Bill and Pete **had left** / had been leaving the airport before I got there.
2 You collapsed just before reaching the finishing line. **Had you been running** / Had you run for a long time?
3 I had sailed / **had been sailing** all morning, so I was feeling very tired.
4 The boys had been packing / **had packed** their bags and then called a taxi.
5 By the time we reached the top of the mountain, the sun had been setting / **had set**.
6 Frank had a headache because he **had been listening** / had listened to loud music since that morning.
7 We hadn't talked / **hadn't been talking** for long before the lights went out.
8 How long **had they been looking** / had they looked for the missing child?

7 Find the mistakes and correct the sentences where necessary. Put a tick (✓) below those which do not need correcting.
1 Yesterday was a very bad day for me because I hadn't been sleeping well the night before.
   Yesterday was a very bad day for me because I hadn't slept well the night before.
2 After Mum made breakfast, we had sat down to eat.
   After Mum made breakfast, we sat down to eat.
3 When she heard the horrible sound, she screamed.
   ✓
4 George hadn't been skiing for long when he suffered a broken leg.
   ✓
5 Did they been waited long before the taxi arrived?
   Had they been waiting long before the taxi arrived?
6 The explorer had been wandering in the jungle for days and collapsed just before rescuers reached him.
   ✓

Vocabulary

Prepositions

8 Circle the correct prepositions to complete the phrases.
1 between / **about** the same size
2 the top **of** / to the mountain
3 **over** / along 32 degrees Celsius
4 onto / **in** a desert
5 **below** / under freezing
6 in / **on** the planet
7 stretched **across** / besides
8 over / **above** sea level
9 during / **over** the years
10 behind / **in** the water

9 Complete the sentences with the correct form of the prepositional phrases from 8.
1 _Over the years_, the explorer had travelled to the four corners of the globe.
2 He had visited some of the most remote areas _on the planet_ – and the earth has some very remote areas!
3 After we had made it to _the top of the mountain_, we stopped to look at the view below.
4 _In a desert_, like the Sahara, days are scorching while nights can get very cold.
5 The child hadn't been _in the water_ for long before she was pulled into the canoe.
6 In countries like Russia, it isn't uncommon for temperatures to be _below freezing_ during the winter months.
7 Tony's feet are _about the same size_ as mine, so he often borrows my hiking boots.
8 We carefully made our way onto the rope bridge that _stretched across_ the river far below.
9 We learnt how far the peak of Mount Everest is _above sea level_; it rises about 8,850 metres!
10 It was _over 32 degrees Celsius_, and I had never been so hot in my life!

Exam Practice

Open cloze

10 Complete the sentences with the word that best fits each gap.

1 ___How___ long had it been raining before it finally stopped?
2 ___By___ the time they had made it to the mountain top, they were very tired.
3 The lost hiker fell to the ground exhausted; he had given ___up___ all hope of being found.
4 I was very angry because my brother ___had___ used my skates without asking first.
5 My aunt had been battling ___against___ her illness for years before she passed away.
6 Mum hadn't ___been___ cooking for long when the smoke alarm went off.
7 I had been struggling ___with___ a difficult decision for ages, so I asked Dad for advice.
8 He had been mountain climbing ___for___ years and was very experienced.

Cloze

11 Choose the correct answers.

1 If I ___ this ordeal, I'll never go hiking alone again.
   (a) survive   **b** die   **c** live
2 It was so cold that we were ___ uncontrollably.
   a crawling   **(b)** shivering   **c** continuing
3 Try, try and try again and you'll ___ in whatever you want to do.
   a overcome   **(b)** succeed   **c** tolerate
4 She had been very badly hurt and doctors didn't expect her to ___.
   (a) recover   **b** persist   **c** achieve
5 Helen had been swimming for years, so she excelled ___ water sports.
   a with   **b** to   **(c)** at
6 If you don't want to get lost, ___ wandering away from the group.
   a face   **(b)** avoid   **c** confront
7 Many retired climbers ___ from lower back pain.
   a vanish   **(b)** suffer   **c** disappear
8 The divers used a cage to protect themselves ___ shark attacks.
   (a) from   **b** for   **c** with

What Do You Think?

Speaking

12 Discuss these questions with a partner:
- What did you do right after you got up this morning?
- What had your mother done before you got home from school yesterday?
- Where had your parents been working when you were born?
- How long had you been crawling before you learnt to walk?
- Had you been going to school for long before you learnt to read?

Unit 14

Awareness

1 Which of these sentences are correct (C) and incorrect (I)?

1. We can borrow the equipment, can't we? C
2. This isn't an interesting course? I
3. She hasn't got any injuries hasn't she? I
4. They're coming to the race, aren't them? I
5. 'Who did win the race?' 'Susan won the race.' I
6. The boat leaves at four o'clock, doesn't it? C
7. Those are expensive uniforms, aren't they? C
8. Let's go for a run, shall we? C
9. 'Didn't Karen come with you?' 'She said she would!' C
10. You warm up before exercising, didn't you? I

How many did you get right? ☐

Grammar

Question Tags

Question tags are short questions at the end of a positive or negative sentence. They are formed with a modal or an auxiliary verb + a personal pronoun.

We usually use an affirmative question tag after a negative sentence, and a negative question tag after an affirmative sentence.
You haven't experienced an earthquake, **have you?**
The rescuers are looking for survivors, **aren't they?**

When an affirmative sentence contains a verb in the Present Simple or the Past Simple we use *do/does*, *don't/doesn't* and *did/didn't* in the question tag.
You go jogging every morning, **don't you?**
You went jogging yesterday morning, **didn't you?**

We use question tags when we want
• someone to agree with what we are saying.
It's a dangerous sport, **isn't it?**
• to make sure that what we are saying is right.
The scuba lesson starts at one o'clock, **doesn't it?**

> **Note**
>
> Some question tags are irregular. Notice the way these tags are formed.
>
> *I am an adventurous person,* **aren't I?**
> *Everyone is coming on the sailing trip,* **aren't they?**
> *Let's take the mountain path,* **shall we?**
> *Don't forget to text me when you get there,* **will you?**
> *Be quick,* **won't you?**
> *This/That is so exciting,* **isn't it?**
> *These/Those are courageous women,* **aren't they?**

Subject & Object Questions

When *who*, *what*, or *which* asks about the subject of a question, the word order stays the same as in an affirmative sentence.
Who survived *last week's boating accident? (***Everyone** *survived.)*

When *who*, *what*, or *which* are the object of a question, the word order changes in the question form.
Who did the **coastguard** *save? (They saved* **a little boy**.)

Negative Questions

We use negative questions
• to express surprise.
Didn't *Stella* **compete** *in the marathon? (No, she twisted her ankle while she was training for it.)*
• in exclamations.
Isn't *he the best athlete on the planet?*
• when we expect the listener to agree with us.
Wasn't *that a boring match?*

To answer negative questions we just use a *Yes* or *No* answer depending on what we think. A *Yes* answer confirms a positive opinion, whereas a *No* answer confirms a negative opinion.
Isn't it a fun sport?
Yes./**Yes,** *it* **is.** (= agreement)   **No.**/**No,** *it* **isn't.** (= disagreement)

Grammar Exercises

2 Circle the correct words.

1 You aren't leaving for the sports camp now, **are you** / aren't you?
2 You've been bungee jumping before, **haven't you** / have you?
3 He'll call me when he gets to Peru, will he / **won't he**?
4 Your uncle hasn't got golf clubs, **has he** / hasn't he?
5 They work out every day, **don't they** / do they?
6 We have lots of time, do we / **don't we**?
7 She didn't give you a chance, didn't she / **did she**?
8 Look at my new snorkelling mask. It's super, is it / **isn't it**?

3 Match the sentences with the question tags.

1 He's never been hiking in the Amazon,   *i*
2 She's a top athlete,   *e*
3 Let's go mountain biking,   *h*
4 Peter can deep-sea dive,   *a*
5 I'm fit enough to go windsurfing,   *f*
6 Don't do anything silly,   *d*
7 Harriet booked her extreme holiday,   *b*
8 Everyone had a great time,   *c*
9 Those people aren't here for the competition,   *g*
10 You've paid for the boat rental,   *j*

a can't he?
b didn't she?
c didn't they?
d will you?
e isn't she?
f aren't I?
g are they?
h shall we?
i has he?
j haven't you?

4 Add question tags to these sentences.

1 Let's do something adventurous, _shall we_?
2 This is the final leg of the journey, _isn't it_?
3 You don't like taking risks, _do you_?
4 Don't leave your flippers in the boat, _will you_?
5 Nancy is frightened, _isn't she_?
6 Everyone is coming trekking, _aren't they_?
7 We should take warm clothes with us, _shouldn't we_?
8 Paul doesn't exercise anymore, _does he_?
9 This isn't very thrilling, _is it_?
10 They didn't have fun canoeing, _did they_?
11 I'm going to win the trophy, _aren't I_?
12 Those aren't expensive trainers, _are they_?

Unit 14

5 Choose the correct answers.

1. Which bike did Sam sell Tina?   b
   - a Tina sold Sam the red bike.
   - b Sam sold Tina the red bike.
2. Who took Pete sailing?   b
   - a Pete took Fran sailing.
   - b Fran took Pete sailing.
3. Who asked Kevin to come on the walking tour?   b
   - a Kevin asked Tim to come on the walking tour.
   - b Tim asked Kevin to come on the walking tour.
4. What was in the rucksack?   a
   - a The water was in the rucksack.
   - b The rucksack was in the water.
5. Who was the coach shouting at?   a
   - a The coach was shouting at the team.
   - b The team was shouting at the coach.
6. What did Lynn buy you?   a
   - a Lynn bought me a new cricket bat.
   - b I bought Lynn a new cricket bat.
7. Who likes animals?   b
   - a Animals like me.
   - b I like animals.
8. What is Sara doing for her trainer?   b
   - a Her trainer is having a party for Sara.
   - b Sara is having a party for her trainer.

6 Write subject questions for the answers.

1. Who plays tennis with Malcolm?
   James plays tennis with Malcolm.
2. Who was teaching basketball skills?
   The instructor was teaching basketball skills.
3. Who went fishing with Dad?
   Francis went fishing with Dad.
4. Who borrowed the blue racket?
   Jan borrowed the blue racket.
5. Who asked Petra to join the team?
   The coach asked Petra to join the team.
6. Who is fixing Jack's net?
   The fisherman is fixing Jack's net.
7. Who took up the most dangerous sport?
   Ted took up the most dangerous sport.
8. Who decided to get the little black puppy?
   The boy decided to get the little black puppy.

7 Rewrite the sentences as negative questions and complete the short answers.

1. You're athletic!
   A: Aren't you athletic?
   B: Yes, I am.

2. It's been an exhausting competition.
   A: Hasn't it been an exhausting competition?
   B: Yes, it has.

3. Adam didn't go bungee jumping.
   A: Didn't Adam go bungee jumping?
   B: No, he didn't.

4. This is the best sport in the world.
   A: Isn't this the best sport in the world?
   B: Yes, it is.

5. That was a great fishing trip.
   A: Wasn't that a great fishing trip?
   B: No, it wasn't.

6. Joanne is an amazing volleyball player!
   A: Isn't Joanne an amazing volleyball player?
   B: Yes, she is.

7. Joey can't ride a bike.
   A: Can't Joey ride a bike?
   B: No, he can't.

8. Those are dangerous sports.
   A: Aren't those dangerous sports?
   B: No, they aren't.

Vocabulary

Collocations & Expressions

8 Choose the correct answers.

1. When you get lost,   **b**
   a. you look for something.
   b. someone looks for you.

2. When you go missing, you   **b**
   a. wish someone was there.
   b. have disappeared.

3. When you save someone's life, that person   **a**
   a. lives.
   b. suffers.

4. When you see results, you   **a**
   a. have improved.
   b. have got worse.

5. When you keep calm, you   **b**
   a. get very excited.
   b. stay relaxed.

6. When you do your best, you   **a**
   a. usually succeed.
   b. often fail.

7. When you make a journey, you   **a**
   a. travel somewhere.
   b. stay at home.

8. When you have a narrow escape, you   **b**
   a. die.
   b. survive.

Unit 14

9 Complete the sentences with the correct form of the expressions from 8.

1. He nearly fell off the cliff. He ____had a narrow escape____, didn't he?
2. Everyone, ____keep calm____! There's no reason to panic.
3. I heard that a group of skiers ____went missing____ in the Alps; I hope they find them soon.
4. All your training has paid off, Joe. I'm beginning to ____see results____.
5. Be careful in the woods. You won't let your sister ____get lost____, will you?
6. It doesn't matter if you win or lose; it's all about ____doing____ your ____best____.
7. The explorers are planning to ____make a journey____ from Peru to Chile. It'll be a long trip.
8. I don't know how to thank you, Officer. You ____saved____ my ____life____!

Exam Practice

Sentence transformation

10 Complete the second sentence so that it has a similar meaning to the first sentence, using the word given. Do not change the word given. You must use between two and five words.

1. We'll get to where we're going before dark, won't we?
   our
   We'll ____reach (get to) our destination____ before dark, won't we?

2. The hiker was lost in the Amazon. He should never have made it back safely, but he did.
   odds
   The hiker was lost in the Amazon, but ____against all odds____ he made it back safely.

3. The Antarctic is well known for its incredibly low temperatures and terrible snowstorms; I wouldn't want to go there!
   conditions
   The Antarctic is well known for its ____extreme weather conditions____; I wouldn't want to go there!

4. The marathon runners had to put up with being incredibly tired and thirsty.
   deal
   The marathon runners had to ____deal with incredible tiredness____ and thirst.

5. Extreme sports make athletes show what they're really capable of doing – and more!
   limits
   Extreme sports test ____athletes to their limits____ – and more!

6. If you want to win at team sports, you and your teammates need to work together.
   co-operation
   If you want to win at team sports, there has ____to be co-operation____ between you and your teammates.

7. The last part of our trip was the best, wasn't it?
   leg
   The final ____leg of our trip____ was the best, wasn't it?

8. You have to be able to endure a lot if you want to trek in the Sahara.
   requires
   Trekking in the Sahara ____requires a lot of endurance____.

Cloze

11 Choose the correct answers.

1. Cyclists should always wear helmets to ___ head injuries.
   a protect   b provoke   **c prevent**
2. The sun in the desert is extremely hot – I hope I can ___ with the heat.
   a cope   b battle   c struggle
3. The trekker ___ to the others that he had spotted a deer.
   a signed   b sighed   **c signalled**
4. The mountaineer had been hurt in a fall, so he ___ when he walked.
   a crawled   **b limped**   c injured
5. The high jumper had been training for too long in the sun and ___.
   a collapsed   b endured   c excelled
6. They say lightning never ___ twice, but I don't believe it!
   a stuns   **b strikes**   c kills
7. It's hard living in a cold country if you're used to the heat, but you'll ___.
   a adapt   b adopt   c adore
8. Extreme sports like sky-diving aren't for everyone; you need to be a(n) ___ person.
   a influenced   b unfriendly   **c motivated**

What Do You Think?

Writing

12 Read the writing task below and write the story in your notebook. Use narrative tenses (Past Simple, Past Continuous, Past Perfect Simple and Past Perfect Continuous), and remember their correct usage!

Write a story which begins with the sentence: '*I had to stay calm or I would never get out alive. ...*'

Unit 15

Awareness

1 Which of these sentences are correct (C) and incorrect (I)?

1	My grandfather can making beautiful things out of wood.	I
2	Can Bill and I go swimming tomorrow, Mum?	C
3	I would take up caving next summer, but I'm not sure yet.	I
4	You should wear a seatbelt when driving – it's a law.	I
5	You really must visit the Louvre; it's incredible!	C
6	Do you think I should get Jake a new camera for his birthday?	C
7	Will you please call if there is a place on the course, Ms Fuller?	I
8	You need to take lots of CDs to the party because I've got a huge collection.	I
9	I'll be able to drive you to the gym tonight, but not tomorrow night.	C
10	You don't have to come, but I think you'll enjoy yourself if you do.	C

How many did you get right? ☐

Grammar

Can & Could

We use *can* + bare infinitive
• to talk about general ability in the present and the future.
She **can knit** lovely pullovers, socks and gloves.
• for requests.
Can we **go** to the cinema at the weekend?
• for permission.
People **can go** into this part of the museum if they pay an extra fee.

We use *can't* + bare infinitive to show that we are sure that something isn't true.
That **can't be** Steve! Isn't he away on a cookery course?

We use *could* + bare infinitive
• to talk about general ability in the past. (past form of *can*)
I **could do** martial arts when I was only six years old.
• to talk about possibility.
We **could go** canoeing tomorrow if the weather clears up a bit.
• for polite requests.
Could you please **take** a photo of my wife and me?
• to make suggestions.
We **could go** to the ballet.

May & Might

We use *may* + bare infinitive
• to talk about possibility in the future.
I **may take** up a hobby in the new year.
• for polite requests. (with *I* and *we*)
May we **borrow** your skis?
• for polite permission.
You **may leave** the classroom when you finish the test.

We use *might* + bare infinitive
• to talk about possibility in the future.
Beverley **might win** an award for her painting.
• as the past tense of *may*.
Dan said that he **might invite** us for Christmas this year.

92

Must

We use *must* + bare infinitive to
- say that something is necessary.

*I **must be** at the art workshop by five o'clock.*
- talk about obligations.

*You **must get** out of the pool when the lifeguard tells you to.*
- show that we are sure that something is true.

*My brother **must be** excited about winning a gold medal.*
- recommend something.

*You really **must go** to the art exhibition! It's amazing!*

We use *mustn't* + bare infinitive to talk about something that is not allowed.
*People **mustn't park** their cars in front of these doors.*

Should

We use *should* + bare infinitive to
- give advice.

*People of all ages **should have** something worthwhile to do in their spare time.*
- ask for advice.

*What **should** I **do** about my stress levels?*

Note

Ought to can also be used to give advice, but it is not usually used in the question form.

Would

We use *would* + bare infinitive for
- actions that we did regularly in the past, but that we don't do now.

*He **would** always **walk** the dog in the evenings when he returned from school.*
- polite requests.

***Would** you please **turn** your head a little to the left?*

Needn't

We use *needn't* + bare infinitive to say that something is not necessary. We don't use it in affirmative sentences.
*You **needn't take** food to the get-together because Mum is making sweets and sandwiches.*

Note

We can also use *need* as an ordinary verb. It has affirmative, negative and question forms and it is usually used in the Present Simple and the Past Simple. It is followed by a full infinitive.

*Mary **needs to get** a better camera.*
*The children didn't **need to walk** to the sports centre because Dad drove them there.*
*Did he **need to buy** tickets for the match?*

Be Able To

We use *be able to* to talk about
- ability.

*I **will be able to come** to your play this evening.*
- a specific ability in the past. (*Could* cannot be used here.)

*She **wasn't able to play** in the band on Friday night.*

Have To

We use *have to* to
- say that something is necessary.

*You **have to practise** playing the piano for an hour a day.*
- talk about obligation.

*We **have to take** a first-aid course before we take the sailing course.*

Mustn't & Don't Have To

There is an important difference between *mustn't* and *don't have to*. We use *mustn't* to say that something is not allowed, whereas we use *don't have to* to show that there is no obligation or necessity.
*In football, players **mustn't trip** each other.*
*You **don't have to play** football with us this weekend if you're too busy.*

Unit 15

Grammar Exercises

2 How are the modals used in the sentences? Choose from the list below.

> advice   general ability in the past   polite request   possibility in the future
> recommendation   something not necessary   something not possible   suggestion

1. That **can't be** my art instructor; he's in Paris at the moment.
   something not possible
2. We **could** go to the new art gallery on Elm Street.
   suggestion
3. **May** I borrow your paint brush, please, Mr Vermeer?
   polite request
4. You **must** see the new play at the Roundhouse Theatre! It's great!
   recommendation
5. I **could** swim when I was only two years old.
   general ability in the past
6. You **ought to** see a doctor about your headaches, Dad.
   advice
7. Mum **may** join the gym next year, but she's still thinking about it.
   possibility in the future
8. They **needn't** pay me for the tickets because I got them for free.
   something not necessary

3 Match the modals with their meanings.

1. **Can** I borrow your pencil for a minute? — h
2. You **must** be at band practice every week. — c
3. You **can** join the photography club. — i
4. You **shouldn't** work all the time. — f
5. You **don't have to** take a gift. — g
6. He **may** have an art exhibition next spring. — a
7. **Could** you clean up that spilled paint, please? — d
8. You **mustn't** talk loudly in the library. — e
9. He **would** always jog in the mornings. — b
10. Do we **have to** wear safety boots? — j

a It's possible.
b It's something that happened in the past.
c It's necessary.
d It's a polite request.
e It's not allowed.
f It's not a good thing to do.
g It's not necessary.
h Is it OK?
i It's allowed.
j Is it an obligation?

4 Circle the correct words.

1. If you have a headache, you can / **(ought to)** take an aspirin.
2. **(Needn't)** / **(Can)** we have our phones turned on in the cinema?
3. Fran **(may)** / should take sculpture lessons, but it's not for certain.
4. You **(must)** / can have a licence to fly a plane.
5. Did the children have / **(need to)** pay for the tennis lessons?
6. We **(don't have to)** / can't go to bed early – tomorrow is Saturday!
7. I **(must)** / am able to have the car back before five.
8. My throat is better, so I **(will be able to)** / could sing in tonight's concert.

94

5 Complete the sentences with these words or phrases, then match them to the responses.

| Can | Could | Do we have to | He doesn't have to | may | must | mustn't | shouldn't |

1 You _____shouldn't_____ work all the time; get a hobby! — h
2 You _____mustn't_____ shout at your teammates! It's wrong! — g
3 _____Do we have to_____ go to summer camp? — e
4 Excuse me, Mr Jenkins. _____Could_____ you help me with my sculpture? — d
5 You _____must_____ wear a helmet when you go cycling or you'll get a fine. — f
6 Hey, Dad. _____Can_____ you give me a lift to the gym? — b
7 _____He doesn't have to_____ take a racket; I've got an extra one. — a
8 I _____may_____ start lifting weights again, but I'm not sure if I have time. — c

a OK, I'll tell him.
b What? Again? Why don't you walk?
c Let me know when you're sure and I'll join you.
d Yes, of course. Give me a minute, please.
e No, only if you want to.
f I know. I'll put it on right now.
g Sorry, Coach. It won't happen again.
h You know, that's very good advice.

6 Choose the correct answers.

1 When I was young, I ___ run for an hour every evening.
  a was able **b would** c might
2 Members ___ use the school theatre without permission from Ms Devon.
  a mustn't b needn't c have to
3 You ___ come early; I'll have lots of helpers.
  a needn't b mustn't c wouldn't
4 She hurt her ankle, but, luckily, she ___ go to hospital.
  a couldn't b may **c didn't have to**
5 ___ you help me with this equipment, please?
  a Need **b Could** c Must
6 You and your brother ___ go to the gallery, but be home by dark.
  a can b might c must
7 After a tough start, Murray ___ beat the other player.
  a was able to b should c could
8 That ___ be our instructor; he's in Scotland on holidays.
  a can't b shouldn't c couldn't

7 Rewrite the sentences using modals. Sometimes more than one answer is possible.

1 You ought to practise more often.
   You should practise more often.
2 She used to walk to the sports centre every evening.
   She would walk to the sports centre every evening.
3 Hey, Joey, is it OK if I use your bike for a minute?
   Hey, Joey, can I use your bike for a minute?
4 It isn't necessary to pay for tickets – it's a free event.
   You don't have to pay for tickets – it's a free event.
5 People are allowed to go into the museum now if they want.
   People can go into the museum now if they want.
6 Why don't we go see the martial arts demonstration tonight?
   We could go see the martial arts demonstration tonight.
7 It's necessary for all players to obey the referee.
   All players must obey the referee.

Unit 15

Vocabulary

Word formation

8 Circle the correct words.
1. Manchester United's support / (supporters) / supportive are the best fans in the world!
2. That man can't be a famous celebrate / (celebrity) / celebration – he hasn't got a bodyguard.
3. Students don't have to (participate) / participant / participation in the music festival, but we would like it if they did.
4. You must go see his sculptures; they're very impress / impression / (impressive)!
5. You didn't see him trip the other player; you should be more observe / observation / (observant).
6. Big Brothers, Big Sisters is an organise / organiser / (organisation) that helps young people.
7. He scored yet another goal and the spectate / (spectators) / spectacle went mad!
8. I must send Tom a congratulate / congratulations / (congratulatory) note – he won first prize.

9 Use the word in capitals to form a word that fits in the gap.
1. All _____participants_____ must have the proper equipment. **PARTICIPATE**
2. I lost the match, but as always my coach was very _____supportive_____. **SUPPORT**
3. In India we saw a painted elephant – what an amazing _____spectacle_____. **SPECTATE**
4. You must come to the party; it's going to be a huge _____celebration_____! **CELEBRATE**
5. If you want to get the job, you should try and make a good _____impression_____ on the interviewer. **IMPRESS**
6. So you won a blue ribbon for your cakes – _____congratulations_____! **CONGRATULATE**
7. You're right. She's an amazing artist; that was a keen _____observation_____ on your part. **OBSERVE**
8. The _____organisers_____ have to be at the concert hall before five o'clock. **ORGANISE**

Exam Practice

Cloze

10 Choose the correct answers.
1. You really should __ time to relax and unwind.
   a spend   b do   (c) take
2. Judo, karate and wado are all examples of __.
   a painting   b drama   (c) martial arts
3. I've always been fascinated __ caves and the people that explore them.
   a in   b on   (c) by
4. I'm a terrible chef; I must take a __ class!
   (a) cookery   b cooker   c cook
5. We could go to the cinema. Are you keen __ horror films?
   a to   (b) on   c for
6. You mustn't __ films or music; it's against the law.
   a surf   (b) download   c install
7. If you want to take up __, you should get yourself a good camera.
   a ballet   b sculpture   (c) photography
8. Stop __ your time; you ought to get a hobby!
   a passing   b using   (c) wasting

Sentence transformation

11 Complete the second sentence so that it has a similar meaning to the first sentence, using the word given. Do not change the word given. You must use between two and five words.

1. This play cannot be missed!
   see
   You _____must see_____ this play!

2. If I were you, I'd make better use of my spare time.
   to
   You _____ought to_____ make better use of your spare time.

3. It's against the law to park in front of the hospital doors.
   not
   You _____must not_____ park in front of the hospital doors; it's against the law.

4. He won because his opponent slipped.
   able
   He _____was able to win_____ because his opponent slipped.

5. I know that's not Picasso.
   be
   That _____can't /cannot be_____ Picasso.

6. You have to have permission to use the court.
   can
   You _____can't/cannot use the court_____ without permission.

7. Dean would come home from work, change his clothes and start sculpting.
   to
   Dean _____used to_____ come home from work, change his clothes and start sculpting.

8. I have a suggestion. How about going to the Moustache Championships?
   go
   I have a suggestion. _____We could go_____ to the Moustache Championships.

9. It's necessary for her to register by 3 September.
   to
   She _____has to_____ register by 3 September.

10. It isn't necessary for you to bring anything.
    have
    You _____don't have to_____ bring anything.

What Do You Think?

Speaking

12 Talk to your partner about:
- two things you must/have to do every day.
- two things you were able to do last week.
- two things you could do when you were five years old.
- two things you don't have to do because you're a teenager.
- two things you may do when you get older.

Unit 16

Awareness

1. Which of these sentences are correct (C) and incorrect (I)?

1	Joseph isn't here. He might not remember our meeting.	_I_
2	You mustn't have spent all your money.	_I_
3	Dad could have been a top athlete, but he suffered an injury when he was 15.	_C_
4	You couldn't have seen my brother at the match; he's touring Asia.	_C_
5	I'm not sure why she was late. She can have been caught in traffic.	_I_
6	I must have be starving – I ate the whole pizza!	_I_
7	If they had asked me, I would have helped clean up.	_C_
8	The coach can't have been angry; he let us leave practice five minutes early.	_C_
9	I can't find my keys. I may have left them in the car.	_C_
10	Peter could have been here by now. Let me text him.	_I_

How many did you get right? ☐

Grammar

May/Might Have

We use *may/might have* + past participle to show that we are not sure about something in the past.
*Tina has got a terrible memory. She **might have forgotten** about our rehearsal.*

Should Have

We use *should have* + past participle to
• show that something we were expecting did not happen.
*Mary **should have made** the team. She's the best player in the school.*
• criticise our own or someone else's behaviour.
*You **shouldn't have stayed** out so late; I was very worried.*

Could Have

We use *could have* + past participle to
• show that we are not sure about something in the past.
*The drama teacher wasn't at our performance. She **could have been** busy.*
• say that something was possible in the past, but that it didn't happen.
*He **could have had** his own art show, but he didn't manage to finish all his paintings.*

Can't/Couldn't Have

We use *can't/couldn't have* + past participle to show that we are sure that something is not true about the past.
They **can't have been** at home last night. All the lights in their house were off.

Must Have

We use *must have* + past participle to show that we are sure that something is true about the past.
She **must have been** out because she didn't answer the phone.

Would Have

We use *would have* + past participle to say that we were willing to do something, but that we didn't do it.
I **would have helped** organise the concert if you had asked me to.

Grammar Exercises

2 What is the function of the modal verbs used in these sentences? Choose from the list below and write a, b, c or d in the boxes.

a ability and willingness to do something in the past, but the action didn't happen
b certainty about the past
c criticism of past actions
d past possibility

1 The drama teacher **shouldn't have criticised** your acting skills – you're only a beginner. `c`
2 I'm not sure, but Peter **might have taken** your helmet by mistake. `d`
3 I **could have put** those chairs away for you – ask me next time. `a`
4 Vincent van Gogh **may have painted** these flowers, but I doubt it. `d`
5 Mum and Dad **could have gone** out to eat, but we're not certain. `d`
6 Stan **would have taken** you to the gym if you had asked him. `a`
7 Dad **can't have made** this delicious pasta; he can't even boil water! `b`
8 Stella **couldn't have won** the gold medal; she's not the least bit athletic. `b`
9 You **must have been** thrilled when your son got into Oxford. `b`
10 You **should have apologised** to Hans – you were very rude to him. `c`

3 Circle the correct words.

1 We can't say for sure, but we think Grant can't / **might** have sculpted this.
2 They **shouldn't** / couldn't have gone onto the ice when they didn't know how thick it was.
3 Your father should / **would** have fixed your camera if he had known it was broken.
4 You **must** / can't have made a good impression on the judges – they're smiling at you.
5 You may / **should** have offered to lend him some money; you've got lots!
6 Karen wouldn't / **couldn't** have driven him to the club; she hasn't got a permit.
7 I **could** / may have been a famous scientist if my parents had supported me.
8 I'm not positive, but I **may** / should have made the football team!

Unit 16 99

Unit 16

4 Rewrite the sentences using may/might have, should have, could have, can't/couldn't have, must have and would have.

1 Tim may forget about the dress rehearsal.
   Tim may/might have forgotten about the dress rehearsal.
2 That can't be Sarah; she left for home hours ago.
   That can't/couldn't have been Sarah; she left for home hours ago.
3 I'll help you move house.
   I would have helped you move house.
4 You should bring some food to the party.
   You should have brought some food to the party.
5 I must be dreaming – fairies aren't real!
   I must have been dreaming – fairies aren't real!
6 Mum shouldn't be so angry with me.
   Mum shouldn't have been so angry with me.
7 I think he may become a couch potato.
   I think he may/might have become a couch potato.
8 Our team can win the tournament.
   Our team could have won the tournament.

5 Match to form sentences.

1 We didn't see Tom at the gym. He — d
2 The door was open when I got home. Mum — e
3 It's getting dark. The children — a
4 You moved all that heavy exercise equipment. I — c
5 You were an hour late. You — f
6 She was a great artist. She — b
7 I didn't hear the phone earlier. I — h
8 Mum and Dad weren't home for supper. They — g

a should have returned from the playground by now.
b could have gone to art college, but she went to law school instead.
c would have helped you do it if you had asked me.
d might have forgotten that we had arranged to meet there.
e may have left the house without locking it.
f should have called when you realised you wouldn't be on time.
g could have had late meetings – they often do.
h must have been in the shower when you called.

6 Underline the extra word in these sentences.

1 We may have <u>had</u> given you the wrong email address.
2 Pam might have <u>had</u> put the tickets in her other bag.
3 Francis should <u>be</u> have known that he can't co-operate with others.
4 That can't <u>to</u> have been the famous painter.
5 He shouldn't have <u>to</u> lied to his mother.
6 Would you <u>to</u> have driven me to practice if I had asked you?
7 We should have <u>been</u> left by now – we'll be late.
8 You shouldn't <u>to</u> have spent all that money – Dad will be angry.

7 Choose the correct answers.

1 We __ have gone to the match, but the tickets were too expensive.
   a shouldn't   **(b) could**   c can't
2 The cookery lesson was cancelled. The instructor __ have been ill.
   a can't   b would   **(c) might**
3 They __ have come to the opening if you had invited them.
   a can't   b shouldn't   **(c) would**
4 Lionel __ have won first prize. His drawing was the best.
   (a) should   b couldn't   c would
5 Tilly __ have lost the game; she was on top of the world when I saw her.
   (a) can't   b might   c may
6 The house is a mess. You __ have wasted the whole day watching TV.
   a couldn't   b would   **(c) shouldn't**
7 Kent __ have got the job; I'll ask him when I see him.
   a would   **(b) may**   c couldn't
8 I __ have been out when you dropped by or I would have heard you knock.
   a can't   b should   **(c) must**

Vocabulary

Phrasal verbs

8 Match the phrasal verbs with their meanings.

1 call for   *h*
2 cut out for   *g*
3 find out   *e*
4 show off   *b*
5 take to   *d*
6 take up   *f*
7 call out   *c*
8 try out for   *a*

a to audition
b to behave boastfully
c to announce
d to start to like
e to discover
f to begin
g to be suited to
h to require

9 Complete the sentences with the correct form of the phrasal verbs from 8.

1 You could have looked online if you had wanted to _____*find out*_____ about the different martial arts.
2 Are you really going to _____*try out for*_____ the main role in the school play?
3 So you're a top athlete – you still shouldn't _____*show off*_____ about the fact that you're super rich.
4 I didn't like ballet in the beginning, but I'm really beginning to _____*take to*_____ it now.
5 You won an Olympic gold medal; this _____*calls for*_____ a celebration!
6 I could have been a rock star, but I wasn't _____*cut out for*_____ life on the road.
7 You're overweight and unfit – you should have _____*taken up*_____ a sport when you were younger.
8 Mary Jane can't have been in the audience or she would have come on stage when I _____*called out*_____ her name.

Unit 16

Exam Practice

Open cloze

10 Complete the sentences with the word that best fits each gap.

1 What do you enjoy doing ____in____ your free time?
2 Tony is obsessed with the stage and he could ____have____ been a great acting coach.
3 I should have listened ____to____ my doctor when he told me to relax more.
4 The writer should have ____been____ here hours ago; where can she be?
5 The Brothers Grimm ____cannot/can't____ have known they would be so famous in the twenty-first century.
6 Have you ever heard ____of____ a fairy tale character called Cinderella?
7 You ____should____ have called when you realised you wouldn't be able to come.
8 The book came ____out____ in 2009 and has since sold millions of copies.

Word formation

11 Use the word in capitals to form a word that fits in the gap.

1 The ____collections____ of fairy tales are still popular with children today. **COLLECT**
2 I'm not keen on video games because I don't think they're very ____educational____. **EDUCATE**
3 His new film is fun and ____entertaining____ for people of all ages. **ENTERTAIN**
4 The book is full of bright colourful ____illustrations____ and lovely little poems. **ILLUSTRATE**
5 The old theatre was ____unrecognisable____ after they had it repainted and decorated. **RECOGNISE**
6 My ____publisher____ feels that I should have written about something that I knew about. **PUBLISH**
7 The children laughed excitedly as the ____magician____ pulled a rabbit out of his hat. **MAGIC**
8 Ever since I was a child, I have had a(n) ____fascination____ with fairies and other 'little people'. **FASCINATE**

What Do You Think?

Writing

12 Read the writing task below and write the article in your notebook. Make your article more interesting by using an eye-catching title and semi-formal language. It's also a good idea to organise your ideas clearly into sub-sections.

You regularly write articles for your school newspaper about new and interesting hobbies. Write an article for the newspaper recommending two or three hobbies that young people may want to take up in their spare time.

Review 4

Grammar

1 Complete the paragraphs with the correct form of the Past Simple, Past Perfect Simple or Past Perfect Continuous of the verbs in brackets. Sometimes more than one answer is possible.

a Two years ago, my grandfather, Jim, (1) ___retired___ (retire) from his company after he (2) ___had been working/had worked___ (work) there for over 50 years. For months after that, my grandpa (3) ___searched___ (search) for something to fill his spare time. He (4) ___hoped___ (hope) to find a hobby that would keep him fit, but as he (5) ___had never been___ (never / be) very athletic he (6) ___knew___ (know) it was going to be difficult to find a sport that (7) ___suited___ (suit) him. Only last week, he called me to say that he (8) ___had found___ (find) a sport he was cut out for – it's a kind of martial art, and he loves it!

b Last August, my family and I (1) ___took___ (take) a trip to Canada. All of us (2) ___had been looking___ (look) forward to our visit for ages and we all (3) ___had___ (have) a fantastic time while we were there. 1 July is Canada Day and my cousin (4) ___insisted___ (insist) that we go to watch the river boat races on the East River which is near her house. I (5) ___had seen___ (see) boats before, of course, but it was the first time I (6) ___had ever seen___ (ever / see) a river boat. What a colourful spectacle! The river boat races (7) ___were___ (be) something I'll never forget!

2 Circle the correct words.

1 Clean up your mess after the painting lesson is over, **won't you** / don't you?
2 A: What was in the bag?
   B: The **water** / bag was in the water / **bag**.
3 I'm going to enjoy bungee jumping, **aren't I** / will I?
4 A: Who invited Brenda to Joe's barbecue?
   B: **Joe** / Brenda invited Joe / **Brenda** to the barbecue.
5 A: You're / **Aren't you** an adventurous person?
   B: Yes, I am.
6 Let's go to the photo exhibition this evening, won't I / **shall we**?
7 A: Which cricket bat did John lend Chris?
   B: Chris / **John** lent **Chris** / John the wooden cricket bat.
8 A: **Didn't Karen go** / Karen didn't go to summer camp?
   B: No, she did / **didn't**.

3 Circle the correct words.

1 If you were bored, you must / **should have** called me.
2 Let's go swimming, can we / **shall we**?
3 Those paints are very expensive, **aren't** / doesn't they?
4 I'm not certain, but I think George ought / **might** be at the pool.
5 Gill **can't** / wouldn't have moved the piano; it weighs a tonne!
6 We don't **have to** / need buy uniforms; the team will provide them.
7 Who did ask / **asked** Van to join the choir?
8 It's / **Isn't it** an amazing play?
9 Until March of this year, I had never been skied / **skied**.
10 Grandpa should / **would** come home and do the crossword every evening.

Review 4 103

Review 4

4 Choose the correct answers.

1. If you twisted your ankle, you ___ to see a doctor.
   a) ought
   b) should

2. ___ eat in the school library?
   a) Are we able to
   b) Can we

3. Dad ___ come parachuting this weekend, but he's still thinking about it.
   a) may
   b) shouldn't

4. My grandmother ___ always work in her vegetable garden in the evenings.
   a) would
   b) might

5. Did you ___ pay for the concert tickets or were they free?
   a) need to
   b) have

6. I ___ make dinner tonight – my husband is taking me out!
   a) couldn't
   b) don't have to

7. I ___ be back before dark or my parents get upset.
   a) am able to
   b) must

8. That ___ be Uncle Joe; he's working in the Amazon rainforest at the moment.
   a) mustn't
   b) can't

9. I had the day off, so I ___ to drive the children to the gym yesterday.
   a) was able
   b) could

10. You ___ wear your life jacket in the boat.
    a) must
    b) could

5 Think about these situations and complete the sentences using *may/might have*, *should have*, *could have*, *can't/couldn't have*, *must have* and *would have*.

1. Your brother can't find his baseball glove. The last time he used it was at the ball park.
   He ___*must have*___ left his baseball glove at the ball park.

2. Your best friend ate an entire pizza. Now she doesn't feel well.
   She ___*shouldn't have*___ eaten so much!

3. It was Sunday yesterday. Your mother didn't work, but she got up very early.
   Mum ___*could have*___ slept in until late yesterday, but she didn't.

4. You went to your coach's house last night. All the lights were off.
   The coach ___*can't/couldn't have*___ been home last night.

5. They went to a party and took lots of snacks. There were already lots of snacks.
   They ___*shouldn't have*___ brought snacks to the party.

6. Your cousin cleaned out his attic this morning, but didn't ask you for your help.
   I ___*would have*___ helped you clean out your attic if you had asked me.

7. Your mother went into your sister's room. She didn't hear her.
   My sister ___*must have*___ been asleep when Mum went into her room.

8. The children aren't home yet. It's after six in the evening.
   The children ___*should have*___ been home by now.

6 Find the mistakes and correct the sentences.

1 The lead racer fell and, as a result, I could win the marathon.
   The lead racer fell, as a result, I was able to win the marathon.
2 The young athlete had swum since she was a child.
   The young athlete had been swimming since she was a child.
3 Everyone from the karate club got a new uniform, don't they?
   Everyone from the karate club got a new uniform, didn't they?
4 I'm not sure, but I must have left my camera on the train.
   I'm not sure but I might have left my camera on the train.
5 All the survivors of the earthquake were allowed to return home, aren't they?
   All the survivors of the earthquake were allowed to return home, weren't they?
6 As soon as they had been hearing the explosion, they raced to the cellar.
   As soon as they heard the explosion, they raced to the cellar.
7 The team had finally been winning a trophy after months of hard training.
   The team had finally won a trophy after months of hard training.
8 You couldn't have eaten all that chocolate – it'll make you ill.
   You shouldn't have eaten all that chocolate – it'll make you ill.
9 That was one of the most exciting things we've ever done?
   Wasn't that one of the most exciting things we've ever done?
10 That mustn't be Jordan; he's spending the year backpacking in Europe.
   That can't be Jordan; he's spending the year backpacking in Europe.

Use of English

Word formation

7 Use the word in capitals to form a word that fits in the gap.

1 If you really try, you can ___overcome___ any problem you might face. **COME**
2 You managed to spot the tiger in the jungle. Aren't you ___observant___? **OBSERVE**
3 Wasn't that odd? One second he was there and the next he had ___disappeared___! **APPEAR**
4 Grant isn't sure; he thinks he may join the ___photography___ club. **PHOTO**
5 You're not a bad chef, but you ought to take a(n) ___cookery___ course. **COOK**
6 Many ___collections___ of the tales have been published since 1812. **COLLECT**
7 We won the championship! Let's have a(n) ___celebration___, shall we? **CELEBRATE**
8 You've decided to take up a sport and get fit – ___congratulations___! **CONGRATULATE**

Open cloze

8 Complete the sentences with the word that best fits each gap.

1 Come on, Marge! You can do it – you mustn't give ___up___ now!
2 Don't get lost now, ___will___ you?
3 Many sports call ___for___ endurance, stamina and strength.
4 Ever since I saw the documentary about Hawaii, I've been fascinated ___by___ surfing.
5 If you find you have a lot of time to spare, you should ___take___ up a hobby.
6 Frank likes sports, but he's not really keen ___on___ martial arts.
7 ___Against___ all odds, the explorer made his way back to the camp.
8 Don't worry about winning or losing – just get out there and ___do___ your best!
9 You're a great actor – you ___ought___ to try out for the drama club.
10 Could you tell us when you noticed that the child had ___gone___ missing?

Review 4

Grammar

For questions 1–10, choose the word or phrase that best completes the sentence.

1. We agreed to take Susie with us, ___ we?
   A did
   B will
   C didn't

2. I'm near the game reserve, ___?
   A am I
   B aren't I
   C isn't it

3. Don't be nervous before you jump, ___?
   A will you
   B are you
   C won't you

4. Tony ___ have been out last night – he didn't answer the phone when I rang.
   A must
   B should
   C would

5. You were late. You ___ to have texted to let me know.
   A should
   B ought
   C could

6. ___ Sue choose to take up?
   A Which did hobby
   B Which hobby did
   C Which hobby

7. ___ a lot of talent?
   A She has got
   B She hasn't got
   C Hasn't she got

8. ___ when you won the gold?
   A Weren't you surprised
   B You weren't surprised
   C You were surprised

9. That ___ be Joe's house – his house is black and that one is white.
   A wouldn't
   B can't
   C shouldn't

10. Gloria ___ come to the concert, but she said she'd call later and say for sure.
    A may
    B would
    C ought

Vocabulary

For questions 11–20 choose the word or phrase that best completes the sentence.

11. Joey, stop showing ___. No one likes people who boast.
    A up
    B off
    C through

12. I'm not going skiing! It's ___ freezing out there!
    A under
    B lower
    C below

13. I ___ a lot of time watching TV – I must get a hobby.
    A take
    B spend
    C use

14. Do you have any idea how far ___ sea level the Asian continent is?
    A above
    B over
    C upper

15. Why have you stretched that rope ___ the river? Isn't that dangerous?
    A beyond
    B onto
    C across

16. I'm exhausted. I don't think I'm cut ___ for cross-country skiing!
    A at
    B out
    C up

17. Vince must have travelled to every country on the planet ___ the years.
    A during
    B over
    C in

18. Janie had been ___ against the disease for many years.
    A struggling
    B preventing
    C battling

19. We enjoy ___ the time talking with friends and family.
    A passing
    B wasting
    C making

20. If I were you, I would ___ foods that make you gain weight.
    A face
    B avoid
    C confront

Unit 17

Awareness

1 Which of these sentences are correct (C) and incorrect (I)?

1. Cars are manufactured in Japan. — C
2. They're following us! We were followed by them! — I
3. An email was sent her. — I
4. By tomorrow, my camera will have been fixing by Dad. — I
5. The assembly line was invented by Henry Ford. — C
6. The papers had been attached with a clip. — C
7. Is the rubbish taken to the dump on Tuesdays? — C
8. The children will be shown the factory next week. — C
9. Many people hurt by falling rocks during the landslide. — I
10. Our computers weren't make in China. — I

How many did you get right? ☐

Grammar
The Passive Voice: Tenses

We use the passive voice when
- the action is more important than who or what is responsible for it (the agent).
*Three windows **were smashed** during the night.*
- we don't know the agent, or it is not important.
*We can use the DVD player again. It **was repaired** this morning.*

The passive is formed with the verb *be* and a past participle. Notice how the active verb forms change to passive verb forms.

Tense	Active	Passive
Present Simple	take/takes	am/are/is taken
Present Continuous	am/are/is taking	am/are/is being taken
Past Simple	took	was/were taken
Past Continuous	was/were taking	was/were being taken
Present Perfect Simple	have/has taken	have/has been taken
Past Perfect Simple	had taken	had been taken
Future Simple	will take	will be taken

> **Note**
> There is no passive form for Future Continuous, Present Perfect Continuous and Past Perfect Continuous.

We change an active sentence into a passive sentence in the following way:

The object of the verb in the active sentence becomes the subject of the verb in the passive sentence. The verb *be* is used in the same tense of the main verb in the active sentence, together with the past participle of the main verb in the active sentence.
*They **are chasing** us! We **are being chased**!*

In this example, we do not know who is chasing us and it is not very important, so we do not include the word *they* in the passive sentence.

> **Note**
> When we want to change a sentence with two objects into the passive voice, one becomes the subject of the passive sentence and the other one remains an object. Which object we choose depends on what we want to emphasise. If the personal object remains an object in the passive sentence, then we have to use a suitable preposition (*to, for,* etc).
>
> *She gave **me** a **mobile phone**.*
> *I **was given** a mobile phone.*
> *A mobile phone **was given to me**.*

Unit 17

By & With

Sometimes it is important to mention the agent (who or what is responsible for the action) in a passive sentence. We use the word *by* before the agent to do this.
*Thomas Edison **invented** the light bulb.*
*The light bulb **was invented by** Thomas Edison.*

Sometimes we want to mention a tool or material in the passive sentence. We use the word *with* to do this.
*The computer **was destroyed with** a heavy stick.*
*The door **was painted with** a new kind of varnish.*

Grammar Exercises

2 Complete the table. Use only one word in each gap.

Tense	Active	Passive
Present Simple	make/makes	am/(1) __are__/is made
Present Continuous	am/are/is (2) __making__	am/are/is being made
Past Simple	made	was/(3) __were__ made
Past Continuous	was/were making	was/were (4) __being__ made
Present Perfect Simple	(5) __have__/has made	have/has been made
Past Perfect Simple	(6) __had__ made	had been made
Future Simple	will (7) __make__	will (8) __be__ made

3 Use the prompts to write sentences using the correct passive form of the Present Simple.

1 cars / manufacture / factories
   Cars are manufactured in factories.
2 hockey / not play / water
   Hockey isn't played in water.
3 books / find / libraries
   Books are found in libraries.
4 tea / grow / Madagascar?
   Is tea grown in Madagascar?
5 folders / save / the memory of the computer
   Folders are saved in the memory of the computer.
6 cheese / produce / Switzerland
   Cheese is produced in Switzerland.
7 computer chips / make / England?
   Are computer chips made in England?
8 songs / not record / laboratories
   Songs aren't recorded in laboratories.
9 the Empire State Building / locate / USA
   The Empire State Building is located in USA.
10 computer science / teach / schools
   Computer science is taught in schools.

4 Complete the sentences with the correct passive form of the verbs in brackets.

1. My computer _is checked_ (check) for viruses twice a day. It's very practical.
2. _Will the food be delivered_ (the food / deliver) to the house by lunch time?
3. The electronic memory _hasn't been filled_ (not fill) yet.
4. Her DVD collection _was stolen_ (steal) last week.
5. While the songs _were being downloaded_ (download), I was watching a film on line.
6. The children _are being taught_ (teach) how to send emails at the moment.
7. It was noon and all the letters _had already been typed_ (already / type).
8. The new CCTV camera _will be installed_ (install) next week.

5 Rewrite the sentences in the passive.

1. The technician installed the program.
   The program was installed by the technician.
2. Silvia hasn't designed a new video game.
   A new video game hasn't been designed by Silvia.
3. The police officer has caught the criminal.
   The criminal has been caught by the police officer.
4. The company will guarantee their electronic equipment.
   Their electronic equipment will be guaranteed by the company.
5. Someone left the computer on all night.
   The computer was left on all night.
6. That scientist didn't develop the software.
   The software wasn't developed by that scientist.
7. Did his sister teach him how to surf the Internet?
   Was he taught how to surf the Internet by his sister?
8. Our employer had told us not to send personal emails.
   We had been told not to send personal emails by our employer.
9. The company is designing a new GPS navigator.
   A new GPS navigator is being designed by the company.
10. Are millions of people using technology?
    Is technology being used by millions of people?

6 Complete the sentences with **by** or **with**.

1. Who was the camcorder invented _by_?
2. The walls of the building were covered _with_ cement.
3. The country roads will be covered _with_ snow in December.
4. The New World was discovered _by_ Christopher Columbus.
5. The lamp shades had been made _with_ silk.
6. The power cord has been cut _with_ a knife!
7. *Great Expectations* was written _by_ Charles Dickens.
8. The remote control is being fixed _by_ a technician.

Unit 17

7 Rewrite the sentences in the passive in two ways.

1 The office supplied him with a new keyboard.
   He was supplied with a new keyboard by the office.
   A new keyboard was supplied to him by the office.
2 Dad bought me some batteries.
   I was bought some batteries by Dad.
   Some batteries were bought for me by Dad.
3 The security company has offered Grant a job.
   Grant has been offered a job by the security company.
   A job has been offered to Grant by the security company.
4 Brett is sending Sam a file.
   Sam is being sent a file by Brett.
   A file is being sent to Sam by Brett.
5 Van will lend Nancy his digital camera.
   Nancy will be lent a digital camera by Van.
   A digital camera will be lent to Nancy by Van.
6 The experts are showing us the microchips.
   We are being shown the microchips by the experts.
   The microchips are being shown to us by the experts.
7 They gave Tim and Bob a lot of money for their invention.
   Tim and Bob were given a lot of money for their invention.
   A lot of money was given to Tim and Bob for their invention.
8 The detective had brought the FBI all the disk drives.
   The FBI had been brought all the disk drives by the detective.
   All the disk drives had been brought to the FBI by the detective.

Vocabulary

Prepositions

8 Complete the phrases with these prepositions. You will need to use some prepositions more than once.

| about | for | in | of | on | to | under | with |

1 communicate __with__ somebody
2 be successful __in__ doing something
3 come __under__ threat
4 look __for__ answers
5 be an expert __on__ something
6 go __on__ safari
7 concerned __about__ something
8 lead __to__ something
9 rely __on__ something/somebody
10 use something instead __of__ something else

9 Complete the sentences with prepositions from 8.

1 The conservationists deal with species that come __under__ threat from man.
2 People have many forms of technology that help them communicate __with__ others.
3 With this new invention, we hope we'll be successful __in__ stopping illegal poaching.
4 People are still looking __for__ answers to solve the world's problems.
5 What will all this crime lead __to__? It's a very worrying issue.
6 I don't like to rely __on__ anyone; I'm very independent.
7 The scientist is an expert __on__ endangered animals and habitats.
8 When we went __on__ safari, we were driven around in a jeep.
9 Are you concerned __about__ the number of closed-circuit TVs there are in the city?
10 Batteries were used instead __of__ electricity to power the phone.

Exam Practice

Open cloze

10 Complete the sentences with the word that best fits each gap.

1 The new equipment ___will___ not be delivered this week.
2 This device ___is___ used for listening to music – here try it.
3 Were fibre optics invented ___by___ Alexander Graham Bell?
4 The hardware had been damaged ___with___ water.
5 The machines are ___being___ powered with solar energy.
6 Helen will ___be___ sent on an IT course in the autumn.
7 The mouse and keyboard haven't ___been___ connected to the computer yet.
8 Before he left the office, a back-up copy of his files ___had___ been created.

Cloze

11 Choose the correct answers.

1 All the data had been saved onto the USB ___.
   a bat   **b stick**   c rod
2 Could you pass me the remote ___, please?
   a control   b power   c energy
3 Once the Internet had been installed, I logged ___, so I could surf.
   a up   b over   **c on**
4 The scientists were conducting ___ until late last night.
   a exams   **b tests**   c exercises
5 Bill Gates, the creator of Microsoft, has ___ the world we live in.
   a developed   b experimented   **c revolutionised**
6 Almost everyone realises that Albert Einstein was a(n) ___.
   a genius   b navigator   c engineer
7 If I had the instruction ___, I might be able to get this to work.
   a gadget   b research   **c manual**
8 Oh no! I think I've just ___ my laptop again!
   a crashed   b smashed   c shattered

What Do You Think?

Speaking

12 Discuss these questions with a partner:

- Are there any CCTV cameras in your town/city? Where are they located?
- What's your favourite gadget used for?
- What inventions have been created since you were born?
- What will have been invented by 2080?
- What technology had already been developed in your grandparents' time?

Unit 18

Awareness

1 Which of these sentences are correct (C) and incorrect (I)?

1 They agreed to being paid for their designs at a later date. — I
2 Bill chose the prizes to be awarded at the science fair. — C
3 Batteries should to be stored in a cool dry place. — I
4 CCTV cameras must be placed everywhere; there's a lot of crime! — C
5 Inventors ought to being well paid for their work. — I
6 Bags must be checked at the front door to the laboratory. — C
7 Proper identification has to be show if the officers ask you for it. — I
8 Applications for the position need to be submitted by 10 June. — C
9 Don't let yourself to be pressured into taking a job you won't like. — I
10 We enjoyed being told stories when we were young. — C

How many did you get right?

Grammar

The Passive Voice: Gerunds, Infinitives & Modals

Tense	Active	Passive
Modal	can take	can be taken
Gerund	taking	being taken
Bare Infinitive	take	be taken
Full Infinitive	to take	to be taken

The computer **should be turned** off before being disconnected from the power source.
She avoided **being chosen** by sitting at the back of the room.
The design had better **be completed** by next week.
This washing machine needs **to be fixed**.

Grammar Exercises

2 Read the sentences and underline all the passive forms.

1 The computer program <u>should be completed</u> today by the technicians.
2 The online crossword is going to <u>be completed</u> by the students.
3 Stella enjoys <u>being read</u> to sleep by her father at nights.
4 Your answers need to <u>be corrected</u>.
5 Solar batteries can <u>be recharged</u> by the sun.
6 Hans resented <u>being lied</u> to by his best friend.
7 The moving features allow emotions <u>to be expressed</u>.
8 The laboratory had better <u>be cleaned</u> today by the cleaner.

3 Circle the correct words.

1 Can films (be downloaded) / being downloaded from the Internet legally?
2 Don't let yourself being confused / (be confused) by the instructions in the manual.
3 We have missed (being taken) / to be taken to the museum by our parents.
4 These tests had better (be done) / to be done by the time I return.
5 The designs were chosen be used / (to be used) in the construction of the new factory.
6 The scientists want their efforts being appreciated / (to be appreciated).
7 I'm really looking forward to my new laptop be delivered / (being delivered)!
8 Your laptop should (be checked) / to be checked for viruses.

4 Match to form passive sentences.

1 The batteries should — *a*
2 I disliked — *f*
3 The electrician risked — *d*
4 Let yourself — *b*
5 They chose his invention — *e*
6 We agreed — *c*

a be replaced every month.
b be entertained by this amazing new virtual reality game!
c to be interviewed by the science magazine.
d being injured when he touched the downed wire.
e to be exhibited at the trade show.
f being told what to do by my colleagues.

5 Choose the correct answers.

1 We can't afford ___ around the city by a guide.
  a being driven
  b to be driven
2 Endangered animals can't ___ on the market.
  a being sold
  b be sold
3 I wouldn't mind ___ for the job in the IT department.
  a be selected
  b being selected
4 Power plants must ___ for safety reasons.
  a be carefully monitored
  b to be carefully monitored
5 The songs ought to ___; they're amazing.
  a be recorded
  b being recorded
6 Some people spend their entire careers ___ what to do.
  a being told
  b to be told
7 The folders have to ___ on a USB stick.
  a being saved
  b be saved
8 The monitor needs ___ with a special liquid.
  a to be cleaned
  b be cleaned

6 Rewrite the sentences in the passive form. Sometimes more than one answer is possible.

1 Can you use this device to turn the TV on and off?
   Can this device be used to turn the TV on and off?
2 We enjoy Mum cooking meals for us.
   We enjoy being cooked meals by Mum.
3 You must plan your project before you begin.
   Your project must be planned before you begin.
4 You had better do your homework before Dad comes home.
   Your homework had better be done before Dad comes home.
5 The inventor wanted them to prove him innocent of stealing his colleague's designs.
   The inventor wanted to be proven innocent of stealing his colleague's designs.
6 You have to ask the professor before you can use the laboratory.
   The professor has to be asked before you can use the laboratory/the laboratory can be used.

Unit 18

Vocabulary

Collocations & Expressions

7 Complete the collocations and expressions with these words.

art   field   hotcakes   market   order   peg   production   top

1. _top_ of the range
2. are selling like _hotcakes_
3. state of the _art_
4. buy something off the _peg_
5. made-to- _order_
6. leads the _field_
7. a buyer's _market_
8. mass _production_

8 Complete the sentences with the correct form of the expressions from 7.

1. Is it Henry Ford who is thought to be the 'father' of _mass production_?
2. This isn't a good time to sell my house; prices are low and it's _a buyer's market_.
3. Looking for a new mobile? Come to *Bell*! Quick! The phones _are selling like hotcakes_, so there are only a few left!
4. We take pride in the fact that all our electronic goods are _state of the art_ – we sell only the latest models!
5. Why wear what everyone else is? Put on one of our _made-to-order_ designs and stand out from the rest.
6. My father only ever bought _top of the range_ products; only the best was good enough.
7. I'm not rich, so I have to _buy_ my clothes _off the peg_.
8. Nowadays, it's Hewlett Packard that _leads the field_ in computers and computer programs.

Exam Practice

Cloze

9 Choose the correct answers.

1. Could you tell me what size ___ I need for this MP3 player, please?
   a microchips   **b batteries**   c folders
2. Some people are against closed-circuit ___ being placed in public places.
   a camcorders   b laptops   **c TVs**
3. ___ cameras are great because after a picture is taken, the photos can be uploaded onto a computer.
   a Electric   b Solar   **c Digital**
4. Oh no! I think I've just ___ my IT assignment!
   a installed   **b deleted**   c stored
5. A lot of ___ has been made in the development of computer technology.
   a protest   **b progress**   c process
6. And the great thing is that the telescope comes with a ___; if it has a problem, you get your money back!
   a quantity   b quarantine   **c guarantee**
7. I've learnt everything I need to know about computers in my ___ technology class.
   a information   b data   c instruction
8. Tony is interested in drawing pictures for advertisements, so he's taking a graphic ___ course.
   a diagram   **b design**   c plan

114

Sentence transformation

10 Complete the second sentence so that it has a similar meaning to the first sentence, using the word given. Do not change the word given. You must use between two and five words.

1 I remember that the teacher told us how to download this program.
by
I remember _being told by_ the teacher how to download this program.

2 Tony is extremely familiar with laptops and the like, so he'll find an IT job easily.
literate
Tony is _computer literate_, so he'll find an IT job easily.

3 They should order new office furniture; what we've got now is antique!
needs
New office furniture _needs to be ordered_; what we've got now is antique!

4 I don't know how this microwave works and I can't find the book that says how to use it.
manual
I don't know how this microwave works and the _instruction manual cannot/can't be_ found.

5 You have to recharge the battery before you use the device.
has
The battery _has to be recharged_ before you use the device.

6 A personal computer needs to be attached to a power source before you can turn it on and surf the Internet.
in
A personal computer needs to be attached to a power source before you can _log in_ and surf the Internet.

7 The computer table was very dusty.
covered
The computer table was _covered with_ dust.

8 When you buy a laptop, the programs needed to work the machine come with the laptop and are not sold separately.
computer
When you buy a laptop, the _computer hardware_ comes with the laptop and isn't sold separately.

What Do You Think?

Writing

11 Read the statement below and write an essay, in your notebook, discussing the arguments for and against this statement and giving your opinion. Begin each paragraph with a topic sentence to introduce the main idea of the paragraph and follow that with other sentences that give examples or support the main idea.

'All public places should be made safer through the installation of surveillance cameras.'

Unit 19

Awareness

1 Which of these sentences are correct (C) and incorrect (I)?

1. Todd said that he was watching a documentary on TV. _C_
2. Pete said that he had been reading Melville's novel, *Moby Dick*. _C_
3. Lyle told that the singer was getting married. _I_
4. My teacher said that she can play five instruments. _I_
5. Nancy said that she was practising her dance routine at the moment. _I_
6. He said that we're going to get concert tickets. _I_
7. Bob and Joe said they had been listening to music all day. _C_
8. She said that we ought to take dance lessons. _C_
9. Bill said he was watching a comedian then. _C_
10. Sally said that her favourite music was jazz. _C_

How many did you get right? ☐

Grammar
Reported Speech: Statements

When we report direct speech, the tenses used by the speaker usually change as follows:

Present Simple	Past Simple
'She **likes** rock and roll,' he said.	He said (that) she **liked** rock and roll.
Present Continuous	**Past Continuous**
'She **is watching** her new DVD,' he said.	He said (that) she **was watching** her new DVD.
Present Perfect Simple	**Past Perfect Simple**
'They **have bought** a new camcorder,' she said.	She said (that) they **had bought** a new camcorder.
Present Perfect Continuous	**Past Perfect Continuous**
'They **have been rehearsing** all week,' she said.	She said (that) they **had been rehearsing** all week.
Past Simple	**Past Perfect Simple**
'He **watched** a documentary on TV,' she said.	She said (that) he **had watched** a documentary on TV.
Past Continuous	**Past Perfect Continuous**
'He **was writing** about *Snoop Dogg*,' she said.	She said (that) he **had been writing** about *Snoop Dogg*.

Other changes in verb forms are as follows:

can	could
'Bill **can** play the bagpipes,' she said.	She said (that) Bill **could** play the bagpipes.
may	**might**
'He **may** come to the cinema,' she said.	She said (that) he **might** come to the cinema.
must	**had to**
'He **must** pay for the tickets later,' she said.	She said (that) he **had to** pay for the tickets later.
will	**would**
'They **will** never like classical music,' she said.	She said (that) they **would** never like classical music.

> **Note**
>
> **1** Remember to change pronouns and possessive adjectives where necessary.
> '**We** are going to put on a play,' he said.
> He said (that) **they** were going to put on a play.
> 'Those are **my** CDs,' she said.
> She said (that) those were **her** CDs.
>
> **2** We can leave out *that*.
> **They said that they** had read the book before.
> **They said they** had read the book before.
>
> **3** The following tenses and words don't change in Reported Speech: Past Perfect Simple, Past Perfect Continuous, *would, could, might, should, ought to, used to, had better, mustn't* and *must* when they refer to deduction.

Say & Tell

We often use the verbs *say* and *tell* in reported speech. We follow *tell* with an object.
The actor **said** they would love her new film.
The actor **told her friends** they would love her new film.

Reported Speech: Changes in Time and Place

When we report direct speech, there are often changes in words that show time and place too.

now	then
'I'm playing the piano **now**,' she said.	She said she was playing the piano **then**.
today	that day
'We're going to the concert **today**,' he said.	He said they were going to the concert **that day**.
tonight	that night
'They can go to the performance **tonight**,' she said.	She said they could go to the performance **that night**.
yesterday	the previous day / the day before
'I saw them live **yesterday**,' she said.	She said she had seen them live **the previous day / the day before**.
last week/month	the previous week/month / the week/month before
'He published the novel **last month**,' she said.	She said he had published the novel **the previous month / the month before**.
tomorrow	the next day / the following day
'I'll get the costumes **tomorrow**,' she said.	She said she would get the costumes **the next day / the following day**.
next week/month	the following week/month
'We're going to the premiere **next week**,' she said.	She said they were going to the premiere **the following week**.
this/these	that/those
'**This** is my record collection,' she said.	She said **that** was her record collection.
ago	before
'I bought that magazine two weeks **ago**,' she said.	She said she had bought that magazine two weeks **before**.
at the moment	at that moment
'He's playing in an orchestra **at the moment**,' she said.	She said he was playing in an orchestra **at that moment**.
here	there
'Your scripts are **here** on the table,' she said.	She said my scripts were **there** on the table.

Unit 19

Grammar Exercises

2 Rewrite the sentences in reported speech.

1. 'I'll get the concert tickets tomorrow,' Lynn said.
   Lynn said _that she would get the concert tickets the next/following day_.
2. 'The lead singer is thinking of quitting the band,' Tom said.
   Tom said _that the lead singer was thinking of quitting the band_.
3. 'He can borrow my guitar,' she said.
   She said _that he could borrow her guitar_.
4. 'We had fun at the cinema last night,' they said.
   They said _that they had had fun at the cinema the previous night/the night before_.
5. 'My dad doesn't like watching television,' Jim said.
   Jim said _that his dad didn't like watching television_.
6. 'The children will have parts in the school play,' Gillian said.
   Gillian said _that the children would have parts in the school play_.
7. 'I have to write these lyrics tonight,' the musician said.
   The musician said _that he/she had to write those lyrics that night_.
8. 'My aunt has been to the Opera House in Sydney,' my friend said.
   My friend said _his/her aunt had been to the Opera House in Sydney_.

3 Julia went on a class trip to an acting school last week and met some of the students and teachers. Report what they said to Julia.

1. I've learnt a lot about the arts. (Jake)
   Jake said that he had learnt a lot about the arts.
2. There are three film studios here. (Mr Francis)
   Mr Francis said that there were three film studios there.
3. I'm finding it hard to learn all my lines. (Patricia)
   Patricia said that she was finding it hard to learn all her lines.
4. The teachers are very experienced. (Candy)
   Candy said that the teachers were very experienced.
5. I'll always be thankful I attended this school. (Hans)
   Hans said that he would always be thankful he had attended that school.
6. We're putting on a huge production next month. (Ms Drake)
   Ms Drake said that they were putting on a huge production the next/following month.
7. I've been busy designing and painting sets. (Kevin)
   Kevin said that he had been busy designing and painting sets.

4 Complete the reported statements with the correct pronouns and possessive adjectives.

1. Tracy said, 'I want to go to the play with my friends.'
   Tracy said that _she_ wanted to go to the play with _her_ friends.
2. 'We're taking our parents to the classical music concert,' they said.
   They said that _they_ were taking _their_ parents to the classical music concert.
3. Janet said, 'I have to get some flowers for my sister, the star of the show!'
   Janet said that _she_ had to get some flowers for _her_ sister, the star of the show.
4. Peter said, 'I'll meet you tonight at the art college.'
   Peter said that _he_ would meet _me_ that night at the art college.
5. Fran and Peggy said, 'We've lost our scripts.'
   Fran and Peggy said that _they_ had lost _their_ scripts.
6. You said, 'I can't audition for your play.'
   You said that _you_ couldn't audition for _my_ play.
7. 'We're going to write our own rock opera,' Bob and Nat said.
   Bob and Nat said that _they_ were going to write _their_ own rock opera.

5 Complete the sentences with the correct form of say or tell.

1 Brenda ___told___ me that she was enjoying her drama course.
2 James ___said___ that he needed a new set of drums.
3 'I'll take you to the show,' Bridget ___said___ to me.
4 Hans ___said___ that he was shocked that he had got the part.
5 Nan ___said___ to me that she was going to the opening premiere that evening.
6 Craig ___told___ the photographer to stop following him.
7 'Meet me at the box office,' he ___told___ them.
8 The director ___said___ to his producer that they needed a break.

6 Circle the correct words and then write what the speakers actually said.

1 Ken told me he **wouldn't**/ will sing my song.
   I won't sing your song.
2 She said that their leading man **had been feeling**/ felt nervous all day.
   Our leading man has been feeling nervous all day.
3 Vince said he **would see**/ saw us at the rehearsal.
   I'll see you at the rehearsal.
4 We said we **were**/ are going to be there on time.
   We're going to be here on time.
5 He said I **should**/ should have take my mum and dad to the concert in the park.
   You should take your mum and dad to the concert in the park.
6 They said that they are going to / **would** introduce me to the writer.
   We'll introduce you to the writer.
7 Mary said she **had to**/ will have to go and see the director.
   I have to go and see the director.
8 Dean said that he **had been**/ has been up all night practising his lines.
   I've been up all night practising my lines.

7 Rewrite the sentences in reported speech.

1 Tony said, 'You ought to rehearse more often.'
   Tony said that I ought to rehearse more often.
2 Billy said, 'This new comedy is very funny.'
   Billy said that that new comedy was very funny.
3 'I'm starting a new novel next week,' she said.
   She said that she was starting a new novel the next/following week.
4 'I got the leading role in the play last week,' he told them.
   He told them that he had got the leading role in the play the previous week/the week before.
5 'I can't afford to buy tickets for the opera,' he said to her.
   He said to her that he couldn't afford to buy tickets for the opera.
6 'This is a very famous theatre,' the tour guide told us.
   The tour guide told us that that was a very famous theatre.
7 'I don't like that actor,' said Francis.
   Francis said that he didn't like that actor.
8 'We may be a little late for the show this evening,' Pete said to Marge.
   Pete said to Marge that they might be a little late for the show that evening.
9 'You had better be more polite to your producer,' he told them.
   He told them that they had better be more polite to their producer.
10 'Those are the photographers who chased me,' the actor said to the police.
   The actor said to the police that those were the photographers who had chased him.

Unit 19

Vocabulary

Phrasal verbs

8 Choose the correct answers.

1. To *turn out* means to — **a**
   a end in a particular way
   b become something else
2. To *get something down* means to — **b**
   a have a nap
   b write something down
3. To *turn up* means to — **a**
   a increase the volume
   b decrease the volume
4. To *sell out* means to — **b**
   a close a shop
   b run out of something
5. To *turn away* means to — **b**
   a let somebody into a place
   b refuse somebody admission
6. To *give out* means to — **b**
   a send
   b distribute
7. To *turn on* means to — **b**
   a switch off
   b switch on
8. To *catch on* means to — **b**
   a decrease in popularity
   b become popular
9. To *act out* means to — **a**
   a perform
   b behave
10. To *grow out of* means to — **b**
    a be too young for something
    b be too old for something

9 Complete the sentences with the correct form of the phrasal verbs from 8.

1. She said that the play ___had turned out___ much better than they had thought it would be.
2. He said that he didn't think that hip-hop music would ever ___catch on___ with older people.
3. 'I think you should ___act out___ the scene a few more times before the performance tonight,' the director said.
4. 'That's very interesting. Let me ___get___ that ___down___,' the interviewer said.
5. 'We have to get the tickets now before they ___sell out___,' she said to me.
6. The teenagers told us that they used to love reggae when they were younger, but that they ___grew out of___ it.
7. 'The club was full and they ___turned___ us ___away___ at the door,' she said.
8. They said they were ___giving out___ free concert tickets for that weekend.
9. 'Don't ___switch on___ the TV; I'm trying to learn my lines,' she said to her brother.
10. She told me to ___turn up___ the stereo because she loved that song.

Exam Practice

Open cloze

10 Complete the sentences with the word that best fits each gap.

1. Grant said ___that___ he had never seen a better film.
2. Tony ___told___ me that he would come and pick me up for the show.
3. The boys said ___to___ their mother that they would be back by five o'clock.
4. Trudy said she was going to a rehearsal ___that___ day.
5. She told me that she had seen the band live ___the___ previous month.
6. He said that he had read the book two weeks ___before___.
7. James told me that the tickets ___were___ there on the shelf.
8. Gina said that they were going to Hollywood the ___next/following___ week.

Cloze

11 Choose the correct answers.

1. I would ___ this film to anyone who likes to be frightened!
   a tell   **b recommend**   c say
2. Ken might not sing or play music, but he's an amazing ___.
   a singer   b musician   **c composer**
3. I love the ___ of this song; they're sad, but wonderful!
   a lyrics   b lines   c script
4. The entire ___ of the play is getting together after the performance for a celebration.
   a actors   **b cast**   c characters
5. They told us we could pick up our tickets at the ___ before the show.
   a stage   b dressing room   **c box office**
6. My dream is to ___ the opening night of a play on Broadway!
   a attend   b release   c clap
7. I don't like ___ like *Big Brother*; I would never go on TV and show off like that!
   a reality shows   b soap operas   c documentaries
8. The ___ is famous for shooting such classics as *Over the Mountains* and *Midnight Dreaming*.
   a filmmaker   b actor   c producer

What Do You Think?

Speaking

12 Talk to your partner about the following and report what he/she said:

- when he/she went to a concert last.
- why music is important to him/her.
- how often he/she listens to music/watches films.
- how many books/magazines he/she has bought in the last month.
- what he/she thinks an actor has to have to become popular.

Unit 20

Awareness

1 Which of these sentences are correct (C) and incorrect (I)?

1. Tina suggested going out to eat. __C__
2. 'When did you record your first song?' she asked. __C__
3. They asked me when did I produce my first film. __I__
4. They asked do I like hip-hop music. __I__
5. Dad promised to drive me to drama practice. __C__
6. Grant asked her if her had written the lyrics. __I__
7. He told me to clean up the studio. __C__
8. 'What time does the play start,' he asked? __I__
9. 'Don't play the music so loud,' he shouted at his son. __C__
10. She asked us take her to the concert. __I__

How many did you get right?

Grammar

Reported Speech: Questions

When we report questions, changes in tenses, pronouns, possessive adjectives, time and place are the same as in reported statements. In reported questions, the verb follows the subject as in ordinary statements and we do not use question marks.

When a direct question has a question word, we use this word in the reported question.
'**When** did you start writing poetry?' he asked.
He asked **when** I had started writing poetry.

When a direct question does not have a question word, we use *if* or *whether* in the reported question.
'Do you like going to the theatre?' he asked.
He asked **if/whether** I liked going to the theatre.

Reported Speech: Commands

When we report commands, we usually use *tell* + object + full infinitive.
'Turn the TV off!' he shouted at me.
He **told me to turn** the TV off.
'Don't touch my iPod!' she said to her brother.
She **told her brother not to touch** her iPod.

Reported Speech: Requests

When we report a request, we usually use *ask* + object + full infinitive.
'Can you lend me your MP3 player, please?' he asked.
He **asked me to lend** him my MP3 player.
(Also: He **asked if I could lend** him my MP3 player.)
'Please don't shout,' he said.
He **asked us not to shout**.

Reported Speech: Reporting Verbs

We use *say*, *tell* and *ask* to report speech (see above).

Statements
•*say* + (*that*) + clause
She **said (that) she had enjoyed** the film.
•*tell* + object + (*that*) + clause
She **told us (that) she had enjoyed** the film.

Questions
- *ask* + question word + clause

She **asked where** the film **was being shown**.
- *ask* + if/whether + clause

She **asked if/whether** we **had enjoyed** the film.

Commands
- *tell* + object + full infinitive

She **told us not to go** to the cinema.

Requests
- *ask* + object + full infinitive

She **asked us to buy** her a ticket for the cinema.

We can also use other verbs such as *promise*, *advise*, *deny* and *suggest* to report speech. Notice the different structures.

verb + object + full infinitive	
promise	'I'll buy you a ticket for the cinema,' she said. She **promised to buy me** a ticket for the cinema.
advise	'If I were you, I would buy tickets for the cinema,' she said. She **advised us to buy** tickets for the cinema.
verb + gerund (-ing)	
deny	'I didn't take your ticket for the cinema,' she said. She **denied taking** my ticket for the cinema.
suggest	'Let's buy tickets for the cinema,' she said. She **suggested buying** tickets for the cinema.

Grammar Exercises

2 Rewrite the sentences in reported speech.

1 'How old is your sister?' she asked me.
   She asked me how old my sister was.

2 He asked, 'Who's that man?'
   He asked who that man was.

3 'Where are your headphones?' she asked me.
   She asked me where my headphones were.

4 'When will you take me out?' she asked Tim.
   She asked Tim when he would take her out.

5 'Can you play the bagpipes?' Clem asked the students.
   Clem asked the students if/whether they could play the bagpipes.

6 'How often do you practise the piano?' the teacher asked me.
   The teacher asked me how often I practised the piano.

7 'What have you done this morning?' my friend asked us.
   My friend asked us what we had done that morning.

8 'Did you go to the concert last weekend?' he asked her.
   He asked her if/whether she had gone to the concert the previous weekend.

9 He asked, 'Whose DVDs are these here?'
   He asked whose DVDs those were there.

10 Nancy asked Pam, 'Do you like classical music?'
   Nancy asked Pam if/whether she liked classical music.

Unit 20

3 Last week, a journalist, Carol Thom, interviewed a famous rap singer, May Lavin. Rewrite the journalist's questions in reported speech using **ask**.

1 'When did you realise you wanted to be a rap singer?'
   Carol asked May when she realised (that) she had wanted to be a rap singer.

2 'Where did you have your first concert?'
   Carol asked May where she had had her first concert.

3 'How many CDs have you made?'
   Carol asked May how many CDs she had made.

4 'Do you write all the lyrics to your songs?'
   Carol asked May if/whether she wrote all the lyrics to her songs.

5 'Do you have to have a manager in the music business?'
   Carol asked May if/whether she had to have a manager in the music business.

6 'Is your life all fun and parties?'
   Carol asked May if/whether her life was all fun and parties.

7 'What do you dislike about being famous?'
   Carol asked May what she disliked about being famous.

8 'Are you planning to go on tour next year?'
   Carol asked May if/whether she was planning to go on tour the following year.

4 Rewrite the studio manager's commands in reported speech.

1 'Keep the door to the studio closed.'
   He told me to keep the door to the studio closed.

2 'Don't come in here when that sign is lit up.'
   He told me not to go in there when that sign was lit up.

3 'Move these microphones to the front of the room.'
   He told me to move those microphones to the front of the room.

4 'Don't touch any buttons.'
   He told me not to touch any buttons.

5 'Don't ask the singers for their autographs.'
   He told me not to ask the singers for their autographs.

6 'Go get us some coffee.'
   He told me to go get them some coffee.

5 Rewrite the requests in reported speech.

1 'Can you lend me some money, please?' she asked me.
   She asked me if/whether I could lend her some money.

2 'Please dance with me,' he said to her.
   He asked her to dance with him.

3 'Please don't play the music so loud,' Dad said to my brother.
   Dad asked my brother not to play the music so loud.

4 'Will you please hold the tickets for me?' Kim asked.
   Kim asked me if/whether I would hold the tickets for her.

5 'Could you give me your autograph, please?' I asked the singer.
   I asked the singer if/whether he could give me his autograph.

6 'Please take your seats quietly,' he said to us.
   He asked us to take our seats quietly.

6 Complete the sentences with the correct form of these reporting verbs. You will need to use some of them more than once.

| advise | ask | deny | promise | suggest | tell |

1 'Your new song is great!' Joel said to the rapper.
Joel _____*told*_____ the rapper his new song was great.
2 'Try listening to music if you need to relax,' said the doctor to his patient.
The doctor _____*advised*_____ his patient to try listening to music if she needed to relax.
3 'When is the show being broadcast?' he said to me.
He _____*asked*_____ me when the show was being broadcast.
4 'If I were you, I would practise more,' the music teacher said to her.
The music teacher _____*advised*_____ her to practise more.
5 'I'll be back before midnight,' Kate said to her parents.
Kate _____*promised*_____ her parents that she would be back before midnight.
6 'I didn't break your drum,' she said.
She _____*denied*_____ breaking my drum.
7 'How about going to the cinema tonight?' Gale said.
Gale _____*suggested*_____ going to the cinema that night.
8 'Let's walk to the concert in the park,' Grandma said.
Grandma _____*suggested*_____ walking to the concert in the park.

7 Change the direct speech into reported speech or the reported speech into direct speech.

1 'What are your plans for the future?' she asked me.
She asked me what my plans for the future were.
2 Joanna denied stealing the MP3 player from the shop.
'I didn't steal the MP3 player from the shop,' Joanna said.
3 Grant told us that he had been chosen for the school band.
'I've been chosen for the school band,' Grant told us.
4 'Turn off that terrible noise,' Mum said to Mary.
Mum told / said to Mary to turn off that terrible noise.
5 'Don't forget to take your instrument to practice, please,' Ms Marks said to Pam and Mira.
Ms Marks asked Pam and Mira not to forget to take their instrument to practice.
6 She asked her best friend to download some songs for her.
'Can you download some songs for me, please?' she asked her best friend.
7 Brett suggested waiting for the rapper at the rear entrance.
'Let's wait for the rapper at the rear entrance,' Brett said/suggested.
8 'I really enjoy your music,' he said to Eliza.
He said to Eliza that he really enjoyed her music.
9 Julia promised her friend that she would take lots of photos.
'I'll take lots of photos,' Julia said to / promised / told her friend.
10 'If I were you, I wouldn't be an actor,' Trish told me.
Trish advised me not to be an actor.

Vocabulary

Word formation

8 Complete the table.

noun	verb	adjective	adverb
(1) _actor_ / acting	act	active	actively
creator/creation	create	(2) _creative_	creatively
(3) _drama_	dramatise	dramatic	dramatically
(4) _entertainment_ / entertainer	entertain	entertaining	–
imagination	(5) _imagine_	imaginative	imaginatively
mystery	mystify	mysterious	(6) _mysteriously_
(7) performer/ _performance_	perform	performing	–
(8) _producer_ / production	produce	productive	productively

9 Complete the sentences with words from the table in 8.
1. You didn't see a fairy! It must have been your _imagination_.
2. I cannot understand how I lost my headphones. It's a(n) _mystery_ to me.
3. Stella is a fashion designer who is famous for her colourful stylish _creations_.
4. He asked me whether the Coen Brothers were the _producers_ of the film *Fargo*.
5. I love Shakespeare and I'm thinking of studying _drama_ at university.
6. She was a great actor, so everyone expected her _performance_ in the play to be amazing.
7. The comedy is fun and _entertaining_ for the whole family.
8. Before he began his _acting_ career he worked as a waiter in a Hollywood café.

Exam Practice

Word formation

10 Use the word in capitals to form a word that fits in the gap.
1. We're so glad we went to the magic show; it was absolutely _spectacular_. **SPECTACLE**
2. 'I'm pleased to see that you're all so _enthusiastic_ about being in the choir,' the music teacher said. **ENTHUSE**
3. I like hanging out with people who are _witty_ and funny. **WIT**
4. We're looking for a few _talented_ actors to star in our new play. **TALENT**
5. I don't think his performance was very _convincing_; I couldn't take him seriously as a pirate! **CONVINCE**
6. She's beginning to take to _classical_ music by composers like Mozart. **CLASS**
7. Look! They're having a(n) _promotion_ for the new *SuperHeroes* film. **PROMOTE**
8. He told us all to be quiet for a minute because he had a(n) _announcement_ to make. **ANNOUNCE**

Sentence transformation

11 Complete the second sentence so that it has a similar meaning to the first sentence, using the word given. Do not change the word given. You must use between two and five words.

1. Kevin said, 'I didn't steal those lyrics.'
   denied
   Kevin _____*denied stealing*_____ the lyrics.

2. 'I'll call you every night that I'm away,' Hans said to me.
   promised
   Hans _____*promised to call*_____ me every night that he was away.

3. 'Get those drums out of my house,' he shouted at me.
   to
   He _____*told me to get*_____ the drums out of his house.

4. 'Could you pick me up after the performance, please, Dad?' I said.
   asked
   I _____*asked Dad if/whether he*_____ could pick me up after the performance.

5. 'If I were you, I'd try out for the band,' Ruby said to Fran.
   advised
   Ruby _____*advised Fran to*_____ try out for the band.

6. The rapper asked us to keep the name of her hotel a secret.
   tell
   'Please _____*don't tell anyone*_____ the name of my hotel,' the rapper said to us.

7. He asked when she had realised that she wanted to be a musician.
   realise
   He said to her, '_____*When did you realise*_____ that you wanted to be a musician?'

8. 'Let's take her to the play for her birthday,' Steve said.
   suggested
   Steve _____*suggested taking*_____ her to the play for her birthday.

What Do You Think?

Writing

12 Read the writing task below and write the letter in your notebook. Try to use clauses of purpose introduced by full infinitive, because + subject + verb, so that + subject + verb, in order to + bare infinitive, etc. to explain to the reader why someone does something or why something happens.

You and the other students at your school often use the gym to hold dances. Recently, the head teacher of the school has said that this must stop because people have complained that the students do not clean up the gym after the dances are over and that there are times when the music is played too loudly. You are a representative of the students and have been asked to write a letter to the head teacher informing him/her about the students' views.

Begin your letter, *'Dear Mr Brown, …'*

Review 5

Grammar

1 Complete the sentences with the correct passive form of the verbs in brackets.

1. My laptop _was damaged_ (damage) when I spilt my coffee on it last week.
2. As we speak, tests _are being conducted_ (conduct) on the surface of Mars!
3. CCTV cameras _are often installed_ (often install) in public places to help prevent crime.
4. These days, many robotic pets _are designed_ (design) by American companies.
5. By 2080, I believe space vehicles _will have been invented_ (invent) that will take us on trips to the moon!
6. In the future, cures for some serious illnesses _will be found_ (find).
7. Some very important data _has been saved_ (save) on this computer – be careful not to delete any of it.
8. Fibre optic cables, which provide us with high-speed Internet, _were being laid_ (lay) in my town all last month.

2 Circle the correct words.

1. My science teacher chose my project to (**be shown**) / being shown at the national exhibition.
2. The batteries for your MP3 player should being recharged / (**be recharged**) every six hours or so.
3. All the lights in the laboratory have to being turned off / (**be turned off**) at the end of the day.
4. This neat little gadget can (**be used**) / to be used for a variety of purposes.
5. He disliked to be asked / (**being asked**) to stay after school and help in the library.
6. Tony let himself (**be talked**) / to be talked into playing in the virtual chess tournament – it lasted for more than 12 hours!
7. The technicians risked be hurt / (**being hurt**) when they failed to wear the proper footwear.
8. We agreed being questioned / (**to be questioned**) about our new invention on live TV.

3 Choose the correct answers.

1. The teacher told them that they should always do their homework. **[b]**
   a 'You should have always done your homework.'
   b 'You should always do your homework.'
2. The workers said the owner would inspect the factory the following month. **[b]**
   a 'The owner will inspect the factory the following month.'
   b 'The owner will inspect the factory next month.'
3. He said the explosion had done a lot of damage in his laboratory. **[a]**
   a 'The explosion has done a lot of damage in my laboratory.'
   b 'The explosion had done a lot of damage in his laboratory.'
4. He said that the library might open a bit late that day. **[a]**
   a 'The library may open a bit late today.'
   b 'The library was open a bit late today.'
5. Lynn told us that the new computers had been ordered the day before. **[a]**
   a 'The new computers were ordered yesterday.'
   b 'The new computers had been ordered yesterday.'
6. She said that gadget was the most useful thing she had ever created. **[a]**
   a 'This gadget is the most useful thing I have ever created.'
   b 'That gadget was the most useful thing I have ever created.'

4 Rewrite the sentences in reported speech.

1 'Can you do me a favour, please?' my sister asked me.
   My sister asked me _if/whether I could do her a favour / to do her a favour_.

2 'If I were you, I wouldn't pay that much for front-row seats,' Yule said.
   Yule advised me _not to pay that much for front-row seats_.

3 'I promise I'll be back from the party by 11 pm,' Julia said.
   Julia promised _to be back from the party by 11 pm_.

4 'Do you like documentaries about animals?' Hans asked.
   Hans asked _if/whether I liked documentaries about animals_.

5 'Clean up this mess!' my mother told me.
   My mother told me _to clean up that mess_.

6 'Don't leave these instruments on the floor!' the music teacher told us.
   The music teacher told us _not to leave those instruments on the floor_.

7 'Where is the art museum?' they asked the tour guide.
   They asked the tour guide _where the art museum was_.

8 'I didn't delete all the files,' Jake said.
   Jake denied _deleting all the files_.

9 'Please take your little sister with you,' Dad said to us.
   Dad asked us _to take our little sister with us_.

10 'Let's go to the rap concert next weekend,' Ollie said.
   Ollie suggested _going to the rap concert the following weekend_.

5 Find the mistakes and correct the sentences.

1 Cory said they had had an amazing time at the music festival last weekend.
   Cory said they had had an amazing time at the music festival the previous weekend / the weekend before.

2 Three people were being injured during the fire at the factory.
   Three people were injured during the fire at the factory.

3 Vince said his father doesn't like soap operas.
   Vince said his father didn't like soap operas.

4 He misses to being cooked meals by his grandmother.
   He misses being cooked meals by his grandmother.

5 I'm given a mobile phone by him the day before.
   I was given a mobile phone by him the day before.

6 The microscope was smashed by a large heavy object.
   The microscope was smashed with a large heavy object.

7 They asked her she enjoyed listening to different kinds of music.
   They asked her if/whether she enjoyed listening to different kinds of music.

8 The moving eyes allow feelings being expressed.
   The moving eyes allow feelings to be expressed.

9 Tracy told to him that she had read the book two months ago.
   Tracy told him that she had read the book two months before.

10 My mother said me to turn down the volume on the TV.
   My mother told me to turn down the volume on the TV.

Review 5

6 Circle the correct words.

1 Those songs had better **being / be** downloaded before I return.
2 Our teacher told us we **were** / are going to the Louvre the **next day** / tomorrow.
3 Can these bottles **be** / to be returned for money?
4 Percy **denied** / promised taking the test results from the lab.
5 Our teacher asked us to please sit down / **to sit down**.
6 We'll be taught how to send emails with / **by** the IT teacher.
7 Ken said I have to / **he had to** learn all his lines that night.
8 Dan told her May started / **had started** cello lessons last / **the previous** year.
9 By 2090, experts **will have invented** / will invent food in a pill form.
10 Mark suggested / **advised** me to join the school band.

Use of English

Word formation

7 Use the word in capitals to form a word that fits in the gap.

1 He told us that Einstein had ___*revolutionised*___ the world with his theories. **REVOLUTION**
2 We're being taught ___*information*___ technology in school this year. **INFORM**
3 He said that he wanted to buy a new GPS ___*navigator*___. **NAVIGATE**
4 The children are very ___*enthusiastic*___ about putting on a school play. **ENTHUSE**
5 I think someone needs to be ___*imaginative*___ if they want to become a graphic designer. **IMAGINE**
6 'The plans have ___*mysteriously*___ disappeared,' the scientist shouted. **MYSTERIOUS**
7 Let's break now for a few ___*announcements*___ from our sponsors. **ANNOUNCE**
8 She said that the ___*performance*___ at the theatre the night before had been amazing. **PERFORM**

Open cloze

8 Complete the sentences with the word that best fits each gap.

1 Wait! Let me get these ideas ___*down*___ before I forget them.
2 'Pick up those papers,' the man said ___*to*___ his secretary.
3 Mum said to me that she was concerned ___*about*___ me becoming a rock star.
4 The names of the winners are expected to ___*be*___ announced shortly.
5 Look at the trees! They're covered ___*with*___ snow!
6 They had run out of tickets and people were being turned ___*away*___ at the door.
7 This manual can be used if you want to be successful ___*in*___ setting up your machine.
8 I don't like hip-hop, but the concert turned ___*out*___ better that I had thought it would.
9 Do you really think this kind of writing will catch ___*on*___?
10 'We're going ___*on*___ safari,' Joey said.

Grammar

9 For questions 1–10, choose the word or phrase that best completes the sentence.

1. Modern technology ___ by millions of people every day.
   A is being used
   B was being used
   C) is used

2. 'The actors from the show will sign my autograph book,' John ___.
   A) said to me
   B said me
   C told to me

3. The burning building was filled ___ smoke.
   A by
   B) with
   C in

4. Ted said that he was listening to some really cool music at ___ moment.
   A this
   B the
   C) that

5. Will a cure for cancer ever ___?
   A) be found
   B find
   C finding

6. 'I ___ that it will never happen again, Professor Graham.'
   A suggest
   B advise
   C) promise

7. Conan denied ___ the telescope.
   A take
   B) taking
   C to taking

8. My teacher told me that ___ song lyrics were very creative.
   A me
   B) my
   C mine

9. After much thought, the technician decided ___ in the project.
   A being involved
   B be involve
   C) to be involved

10. The tourist asked us where the Library of Congress ___.
    A has been
    B is
    C) was

Vocabulary

10 For questions 11–20, choose the word or phrase that best completes the sentence.

11. These tickets are selling like ___; get yours today!
    A) hotcakes
    B pies
    C biscuits

12. The actors stood at the front of the ___ and listened happily to the applause.
    A dressing room
    B box office
    C) stage

13. He told the interviewer that a lot of ___ had been made in solving the problem.
    A) progress
    B research
    C data

14. 'Can you believe I have to learn this whole ___ by tomorrow?' she said.
    A lyrics
    B) script
    C lines

15. The ___ was about the NASA space programme.
    A) documentary
    B soap opera
    C reality show

16. 'Oh no! I think my computer has ___; the screen is blank!' he told me.
    A) crashed
    B logged in
    C installed

17. The scene was acted out by two of the best ___ in show business.
    A entertain
    B) entertainers
    C entertaining

18. 'I'm computer ___, so I'm perfect for the position in the IT department,' he said.
    A) literate
    B intelligent
    C smart

19. This camcorder is ___ of the art – you won't find a newer model anywhere.
    A range
    B) state
    C mass

20. A ___ of Cinderella is being shown at the theatre this evening.
    A producer
    B produce
    C) production

Unit 21

Awareness

1 Which of these sentences are correct (C) and incorrect (I)?

1. They weren't having their house painted all last week. _C_
2. Was Bill having his grass cut yesterday evening? _C_
3. My parents have had a party arranged for them by a caterer. _C_
4. Gina had her tyres slashed a vandal last month. _I_
5. We have been had the morning paper delivered since we moved into this flat. _I_
6. I'm operating on my leg later today. _I_
7. The students will having their papers graded at the weekend. _I_
8. My sister and I getting our rooms decorated at the moment. _I_
9. The school is getting all new computers installed next year. _C_
10. We had had a meal prepared for us at our table. _C_

How many did you get right? ☐

Grammar
Causative

We use the causative to
• say that someone has arranged for somebody to do something for them.
*Sheila **is having her hair cut** this afternoon.*
• say that something unpleasant happened to someone.
*Ms Jones **has had her window broken**.*

We form the causative with *have* + object + past participle. It can be used in a variety of tenses.
*They **were having their curtains hung** last week.*
*Uncle Pete **has been having his suits made** for him for years.*
*The school **has its floors waxed** every month.*

Note

We can also use *get* + object + past participle. This structure is less formal.
*Pat **got his iPod stolen** on the train yesterday!*

Grammar Exercises

2 Tick (✓) the sentences that use the causative.

1. Karen is painting her nails. ☐
2. Tim wasn't having his car repaired. ✓
3. Are they having a pool installed? ✓
4. The bride has been having her dress designed. ✓
5. Hans had been having his tooth filled when he screamed in pain. ✓
6. The farmer had harvested all his crops. ☐
7. The school will have all the classrooms cleaned. ✓
8. The vandal sprayed graffiti on the park benches. ☐

3 **Circle the correct words to form sentences in the causative.**

1 They (won't be having the school supplies delivered) / won't deliver the school supplies until later in the week.
2 Tom (had his tyres checked) / checked his tyres last night.
3 A vet is examining my dog / (I'm having my dog examined by a vet) at the moment.
4 Are the Morgans (having their garden designed) / designing their garden by professionals?
5 She (has her children looked after) / looks after her children every weekday.
6 Jake will cut down the tree / (will have the tree cut down) next month.
7 The students (have been having uniforms made) / have been making uniforms for the past few days.
8 He (had had his film developed) / had developed his film after he got back from summer holidays.

4 **Complete the sentences with the correct causative form of the verbs in brackets.**

1 _Have they had the pizza delivered_ (they / the pizza / deliver) yet? I'm starving!
2 As soon as we _have had our flat painted_ (our flat / paint), we'll move in.
3 The school _had its newspaper printed_ (its newspaper / print) last Monday.
4 Tomorrow they _are having new blackboards installed_ (new blackboards / install) in the secondary school.
5 We _haven't had our compositions corrected_ (not / our compositions / correct) by the teacher yet.
6 Mum and Dad _will have had the fence repaired_ (the fence / repair) by the end of the summer.
7 Frannie _is having her hair dyed_ (her hair / dye) by the hairdresser tomorrow morning.
8 They _were having their central heating fixed_ (their central heating / fix) when she called them last night.

5 **Find the mistakes and correct the sentences where necessary. Put a tick (✓) below those which do not need correcting.**

1 Benny got his bike stole from outside the school yesterday.
   Benny got his bike stolen from outside the school yesterday.
2 Lynn is get her graduation gown taken in at the moment.
   Lynn is getting her graduation gown taken in at the moment.
3 They were have the windows replaced when it began to snow.
   They were having the windows replaced when it began to snow.
4 Did Peter getting his kitchen cupboards replaced when you visited him?
   Was Peter getting his kitchen cupboards replaced when you visited him?
5 Tonia got her shop windows broken the night before.
   ✓
6 Bridget had had her handbag stolen, so she went to the police station.
   ✓
7 My sister has her leg broken while she was on a school skiing trip.
   My sister had her leg broken while she was on a school skiing trip.
8 The teachers are getting lists of their students names photocopy.
   The teachers are getting lists of their students' names photocopied.

Unit 21 133

Unit 21

6 Read about the people in the sentences and then answer the questions. Use the causative. Sometimes more than one answer is possible.

1. The doctor is testing Billy's hearing. What is Billy doing?
   He's having his hearing tested.
2. This time tomorrow a photographer will be taking the students' photographs. What will the students be doing?
   The students will be having their photographs taken by a photographer.
3. Dean's computer crashed, so a technician fixed it. What did Dean do?
   Dean had his computer fixed by a technician.
4. If Sarah doesn't wear a helmet when she goes cycling, her parents will take away her bike. What will happen to her?
   Sarah will have her bike taken away from her by her parents.
5. You fell during football practice and you hurt your knee. Your coach said a doctor must examine it. What must you do?
   You must have your knee examined by a doctor.
6. Interior designers were decorating the flat for me all day yesterday. What was I doing?
   I was having my flat decorated by interior designers.
7. An electrician is changing a light bulb because it burnt out. What are we doing at the moment?
   We are having a light bulb changed by an electrician.
8. The head teacher will ask his secretary to send his emails. What will the head teacher do?
   The head teacher will have his emails sent by his secretary.

7 Rewrite the sentences using the causative.

1. Jude's housekeeper washes all his clothes.
   Jude has all his clothes washed by his housekeeper.
2. The students' homework will be checked by the teacher.
   The students will have their homework checked by the teacher.
3. The lawyer was preparing Jim's new contract.
   Jim was having his new contract prepared by the lawyer.
4. They used to have someone repair the roof every autumn.
   They had the roof repaired every autumn.
5. Did the technician download the computer program for you?
   Did you have the computer program downloaded for you by the technician?
6. My house was vandalised last Wednesday night.
   I had my house vandalised last Wednesday night.
7. Did the shop deliver the flowers to her office?
   Did they have the flowers delivered to her office by the shop?
8. Mum is going to arrange for someone to plant some trees.
   Mum is going to have some trees planted.

Vocabulary

Collocations & Expressions

8 Circle the correct words to complete the collocations and expressions.
1 get / have / (be) a bookworm
2 burn / (break) / get the rules
3 (be) / make / have in the teacher's good books
4 make / take / (get) the hang of something
5 be / (make) / break progress
6 break / make / (burn) the candle at both ends
7 do / (get) / make a taste for something
8 (make) / do / try an effort

9 Complete the sentences with the correct form of the expressions from 8.
1 Tony is always exhausted at exam time; he's a student and a part-time chef, so he has to ___burn the candle at both ends___ to keep up with everything.
2 I got all 'A's on my final exams; I'll ___be in the teacher's good books___ now!
3 I don't think you spent any time on this project at all. Why don't you ___make an effort___ to do better, Stan?
4 I'm having the maths teacher show me how to do these equations and I'm slowly ___getting the hang of___ how they're done.
5 My little brother ___is a bookworm___; he always has his nose buried in a novel or a magazine of some kind.
6 If you ___break the rules___, you'll be sent to the head teacher to be punished.
7 You got a 'B' for your English composition, Stella. You ___have made progress___ in my class – well done!
8 We didn't like Japanese food when we first move to Tokyo, but we ___are getting a taste for/got a taste for___ it.

Exam Practice

Cloze

10 Choose the correct answers.
1 My sister has her university __ paid by my parents.
   a applications   b grants   (c) fees
2 Professor Oakes is the best __ in the college; there are queues of students when he gives a talk.
   a tutor   b graduate   (c) lecturer
3 As far as I'm concerned, nothing is more important in life than a good __.
   a knowledge   b test   (c) education
4 Could you put these books in your __ for me? I'll get them later.
   a schedule   (b) backpack   c timetable
5 Do students have to wear __ at your secondary school?
   (a) uniforms   b folders   c staplers
6 Students must have their __ graded by no later than 31 January.
   (a) projects   b diplomas   c certificates
7 Is your brother completing his __ at the local college?
   (a) studies   b arts   c sciences
8 I was in my __ class and I twisted my ankle playing basketball.
   a biology   b chemistry   (c) physical education

Unit 21 135

Unit 21

Sentence transformation

11 Complete the second sentence so that it has a similar meaning to the first sentence, using the word given. Do not change the word given. You must use between two and five words.

1. They arranged for the school bulletin to be printed last week.
   had
   They _____had the school bulletin printed_____ last week.

2. A dog tore my trousers this morning.
   got
   I _____got my trousers torn by_____ a dog this morning.

3. A thief broke into my dad's car last night.
   broken
   My dad _____had/got his car broken into_____ last night by a thief.

4. Someone is explaining the exercise to Stella.
   is
   Stella _____is having the exercise explained_____ to her.

5. Vince pays someone to shine his shoes every morning.
   gets
   Vince _____gets his shoes shined_____ every morning.

6. She employed someone who will lay the carpets in her new flat.
   have
   She _____'ll have the carpets laid_____ in her new flat.

7. Petra's eye was blackened in the accident.
   had
   Petra _____had her eye blackened_____ in the accident.

8. They'll take your laptop away if you use it to cheat on the test.
   taken
   You _____'ll have your laptop taken_____ away if you use it to cheat on the test.

What Do You Think?

Speaking

12 Discuss these questions with a partner:
- What do you have done for you on a daily basis?
- What did your parents have done to your house/flat in the last year?
- What will your school have done during the school year?
- What are you having done for you today?
- What did your teacher get you do for him/her last week?
- Have you had anything unpleasant done to you recently?

Unit 22

Awareness

1 Which of these sentences are correct (C) and incorrect (I)?

1 Joey is very bad at do maths equations. — *I*
2 They regret not making the best of their years at university. — *C*
3 It's not worth arguing with the teacher; she'll make you sit the test. — *C*
4 Book reports can handed in at the end of this week. — *I*
5 They went to the laboratory to do an experiment. — *C*
6 I was sad hearing the news that you had failed. — *I*
7 He wasn't tall enough to play in the school basketball team. — *C*
8 You'd better tell the coach if you're going to be late for practice. — *C*
9 We'd rather to take the bus than walk to school. — *I*
10 Mum and Dad persuaded me going to university. — *I*

How many did you get right? ☐

Grammar

Gerunds

We form gerunds with verbs and the *-ing* ending.
We can use gerunds
• as nouns.
Cycling *is my favourite sport.*
Tonia likes **skateboarding**.
• after prepositions.
Ken's only six, but he's very good **at counting**.
• after the verb *go* when we talk about activities.
My family **is going skiing** *at the weekend.*

We also use gerunds after certain verbs and phrases.

admit	feel like	like
avoid	forgive	love
be used to	hate	miss
can't help	have difficulty	practise
can't stand	imagine	prefer
deny	involve	prevent
dislike	it's no good	regret
(don't) mind	it's no use	risk
enjoy	it's (not) worth	spend time
finish	keep	suggest
fancy		

Some students **have been spending time decorating** *the gym for the dance.*
I **don't feel like studying** *for my exams. I'll be glad when they are over!*

Infinitives

	Active	Passive
Present	(to) **read**	(to) **be read**
Perfect	(to) **have read**	(to) **have been read**

The teacher threatened **to send** *the badly-behaved student to the head teacher.*
Photos can **be uploaded** *onto my laptop.*
You should **have studied** *more for your maths test.*
He should **have been expelled** *from school.*

Unit 22

Full Infinitives

We form full infinitives with *to* and the verb. We use full infinitives
• to explain purpose.
*They logged onto the Internet **to do** some research for tomorrow's class.*
• after adjectives such as *afraid, scared, happy, glad, sad,* etc.
*Ted was **afraid to go** to the head teacher's office.*
• after the words *too* and *enough*.
*It is **too** early **to know** what he wants to do after he graduates.*
*His project wasn't good **enough** for him **to win** a prize.*

We also use full infinitives after certain verbs and phrases.

afford	ask	fail	manage	prepare	start
agree	begin	forget	need	pretend	want
allow	choose	hope	offer	promise	would like
appear	decide	invite	persuade	refuse	
arrange	expect	learn	plan	seem	

*The students **would like to give** their teacher a gift at the retirement party.*

Bare Infinitives

We use bare infinitives after
• modal verbs.
*You **should go** to the Career's Day to get some ideas about what you can do in the future.*
• *had better* to give advice.
*You**'d better get** some extra help if you're having difficulties with your studies.*
• *would rather* to talk about preference. We often use the word *than*.
*We**'d rather watch** a film than listen to music.*

Gerund or Infinitive?

Some verbs can be followed by a gerund or a full infinitive with no change in meaning. Some common verbs are *begin, bother, continue, hate, like, love* and *start*.
*The students began **cleaning / to clean** the classroom at ten o'clock.*
*Joe knew he would fail the test, so he didn't bother **studying / to study** for it.*
*Ms Marks continued **speaking / to speak** until the bell sounded.*
*Teenagers love **hanging out / to hang out** with their friends.*
*Don't start **writing / to write** until I tell you to.*

There are other verbs that can be followed by a gerund or a full infinitive, but the meaning changes. Some common ones are *regret, forget, go on, remember, stop* and *try*.
*I **regret going** to a local college.* (I went to a local college, but now I wish I hadn't.)
*I **regret to tell** you that you've failed both of the exams.* (I'm sorry that I have to give you this news.)
*Kate **forgot putting** her books in her locker and went home without them.* (She didn't remember that she had put her books in her locker, and she went home without them.)
*Stella **forgot to pick up** the tickets, and she missed the match.* (Stella didn't remember she had to pick up the tickets and so she missed the match.)
*Coach McLeod **went on talking** about good sportsmanship for ages!*
(He continued to talk about the same thing.)
*Coach McLeod **went on to talk** about good sportsmanship.* (He had been talking about a different subject, and then started talking about a new subject – good sportsmanship.)
*My mother **remembers learning** algebra in primary school.* (She learnt algebra in primary school and now she remembers learning it.)
*My mother **remembered to make** me a sandwich for lunch.* (She remembered first and then made me a sandwich for lunch.)
*I **stopped going** to the chess club.* (I don't go to the chess club any more.)
*I **stopped to watch** the documentary.* (I stopped doing something else, so I could start to watch the documentary.)
*If you can't concentrate very easily, **try studying** with the radio on.* (You can study with the radio on, but it might not help you.)
*If you're new at the school, **try to meet** as many of your classmates as you can.* (You might not be able to meet them all.)

Grammar Exercises

2 Circle the correct words.
1. Jake's favourite pastime is **rollerblading** / to rollerblade.
2. You know, you're good enough play / **to play** in the national team!
3. I would like **to know** / knowing why you haven't done your homework!
4. Come on. I don't mind to drive / **driving** you to band practice.
5. Joyce should have been **expelled** / expelling for her terrible behaviour.
6. If you don't mind, I think I'd rather being / **be** alone right now.
7. I'm not very good at do / **doing** crossword puzzles.
8. My friends and I are going cycle / **cycling** this evening.
9. We prefer **studying** / study in the school library.
10. Hank logged onto the Internet surfing / **to surf**.

3 Match to form sentences.
1. I spend a lot of time — *e*
2. We've arranged — *c*
3. Tony loves — *g*
4. Don't start — *d*
5. She can't stand — *a*
6. It's no good — *h*
7. You'd better — *b*
8. I forgot — *f*

a. living on her own.
b. apologise to your teacher for being late.
c. to go to Paris on a school trip this year.
d. running until you hear the starting gun.
e. hanging out in the park with my friends – I love it!
f. to get some eggs and flour on my way home.
g. playing chess in his spare time.
h. crying over spilt milk, is it?

4 Choose the correct answers.
1. You'd better ___ a good night's sleep; you've got a big day tomorrow.
   a. getting   **b. get**   c. to get
2. Dad can't help ___ at you when you don't try to do better at school.
   a. yelling   b. to yell   c. yell
3. Applications for the course can ___ on line.
   a. be completed   b. to be completed   c. completed
4. She called me ___ what we had for homework.
   a. asking   b. ask   **c. to ask**
5. Brett admitted ___ on his final exam.
   a. to cheat   b. cheat   **c. cheating**
6. Are you used to ___ with all the lights on?
   a. sleep   **b. sleeping**   c. to sleep
7. I was so afraid ___ to her for help, but now I'm glad I did.
   a. to go   b. going   c. go
8. The test seemed ___ easy, but the whole class ended up failing it.
   a. to be   b. being   c. be

Unit 22

5 Complete the sentences with the full infinitive or -ing form of the verbs in brackets.
1. Kyle will never forget ___canoeing___ (canoe) through the Snake River Canyon.
2. I remember ___eating___ (eat) apple pie in my grandmother's kitchen when I was young.
3. I regret ___taking___ (take) her pencil without asking her first.
4. First the lecturer talked about poetry and then she went on ___to discuss___ (discuss) novel writing.
5. Patricia stopped ___going___ (go) on holidays with her parents last year.
6. We regret ___to inform___ (inform) you that your plane has been delayed.
7. Oh no. I forgot ___to do___ (do) my homework assignment!
8. The flowers were so pretty that we stopped ___to smell___ (smell) them.
9. The teacher went on ___shouting___ (shout) about how lazy we were for hours!
10. Luckily, Vince remembered ___to buy___ (buy) his wife a gift for their anniversary.

6 Complete the sentences about you. Use the correct infinitive or -ing form.
1. I'd rather ___Students' own answers___ .
2. I often have difficulty _____ .
3. My friends and I dislike _____ .
4. I sometimes go to the library _____ .
5. I miss _____ .
6. My classmates and I spend a lot of time _____ .
7. I remember _____ .
8. I'm too _____ .
9. I can't afford _____ .
10. My family may _____ .

7 Complete the sentences with the correct infinitive or -ing form of the verbs in brackets.
1. You don't have to thank me; I was more than happy ___to help___ (help).
2. Why do you keep on ___wearing___ (wear) my clothes without asking me?
3. I can't believe it! I've been invited ___to go___ (go) to the graduation party.
4. It took a lot of hard work, but we finally managed ___to finish___ (finish) the project.
5. Does your daughter plan ___to travel___ (travel) when she completes her studies?
6. When your room is clean you're allowed ___to spend___ (spend) time with your friends.
7. I'm afraid your son's grades aren't good enough for the university ___to accept___ (accept) him.
8. You should ___stop___ (stop) complaining and just do what you have to do.
9. If you insist on ___cycling___ (cycle) without a helmet, you risk ___getting___ (get) injured.
10. Why are you pretending ___to do___ (do) research? I know you turned the computer on ___to surf___ (surf) the Internet.

Vocabulary

Prepositions

8 Complete the phrases with these prepositions. You will need to use some of the prepositions more than once.

| about | at | for | from | in | of | on | with |

1. to apply ___for___ something
2. a place ___at___ university
3. to suffer ___from___ something
4. an increase ___in___ something
5. to concentrate ___on___ something
6. to spend money ___on___ something
7. ___at___ a certain age
8. to be bad ___at___ something
9. large amounts ___of___ something
10. to worry ___about___ something
11. to be good ___at___ something
12. to be satisfied ___with___ something

9 Complete the sentences with the correct prepositions from 8.

1 If I were as good ___at___ acting as Dean, I'd go to drama school.
2 You may be satisfied ___with___ your grades, but I think you can do much better.
3 Greta is a great girl, but she suffers ___from___ shyness and so she has few friends.
4 Did you know that Pete is thinking about applying ___for___ a position at the college?
5 Tom left home ___at___ 18 and set out to explore the world.
6 I hope to get a place ___at___ Harvard University; I've got my fingers crossed!
7 If I need to concentrate ___on___ something, I always turn the radio on.
8 You shouldn't leave large amounts ___of___ cash in your flat.
9 How can anyone spend as much money ___on___ books as Helen does?
10 There has been an increase ___in___ the number of students being expelled.
11 Kate is really bad ___at___ skiing, but she still goes every weekend.
12 Calm down, Megan. There's no use worrying ___about___ it until it happens.

Exam Practice

Open cloze

10 Complete the sentences with the word that best fits each gap.

1 If you don't know the meaning of a word, ___use___ a dictionary.
2 Your papers must ___be___ handed in at the end of this hour.
3 We ___would___ rather stay in than go out tonight.
4 It's cold outside; you ___had___ better wear a jacket.
5 This appears ___to___ be Joe's writing, but I can't be sure.
6 These equations are ___too___ difficult for her to do.
7 If you don't answer all the questions on the exam, you ___lose___ marks.
8 I can't believe I got an 'F'! I've never ___failed___ a test before.

Word formation

11 Use the word in capitals to form a word that fits in the gap.

1 Hello. I'm interested in taking an IT course – when do ___enrolments___ start? **ENROL**
2 If my brother doesn't get a(n) ___scholarship___, he won't be able to afford to go to university. **SCHOLAR**
3 Juan has just moved here from Cuba, so his ___pronunciation___ still needs some work. **PRONOUNCE**
4 What are you planning to wear to the ___graduation___ party? **GRADUATE**
5 Is Tina in primary or ___secondary___ school this year? **SECOND**
6 Once I give you your homework ___assignments___, you are allowed to leave. **ASSIGN**
7 I regret to tell you that you don't have the right ___qualifications___ for the job. **QUALIFY**
8 Make sure you greet the ___examiner___ politely when you enter the room. **EXAM**

What Do You Think?

Writing

12 Read the writing task below and write the report in your notebook. Try to use words like both, either and neither in their correct forms to talk about two people or things.

You recently carried out a student survey on the sports facilities at your school as part of your physical education project. Write a report summarising opinions on two facilities mentioned in the survey and suggest how these facilities could be improved.

Unit 23

Awareness

1 Which of these sentences are correct (C) and incorrect (I)?

1. Do you like my French cotton new scarf? — I
2. Tony is tired; he has been working in the laboratory all day. — C
3. This course is bored; I wish I hadn't taken it. — I
4. We visit our grandparents regularly. — C
5. Diane last week graduated from medical college. — I
6. Tom is quite good at solving puzzles. — C
7. Grant isn't intelligent enough to get into Oxford University. — C
8. My dream is to live in a lovely little wooden cabin by the sea. — C
9. Dan placed gently the child on the bed after it had fallen asleep. — I
10. It was so a nice day that we decided to go swimming. — I

How many did you get right? ☐

Grammar

Order of Adjectives

When we use two or more adjectives to describe something or someone, we usually put them in a certain order. Notice the correct order.

opinion	size	age	shape	colour	origin	material	
nice	small	old	round	pink	French	cotton	**noun**
beautiful	large	new	oval	beige	Italian	wooden	
strong	big	ancient	long	white	Japanese	silk	

He has **nice short red** hair.
Why does he always wear those **ugly orange polyester** trousers when he goes golfing?
We are staying in a **big modern Swiss** chalet.

Adjectives ending in -ed & -ing

Adjectives that end in *-ed* describe how someone feels whereas adjectives that end in *-ing* describe a person, place or thing.
She's **interested** in animals and their health and she wants to be a vet.
This article on raising animals is very **interesting**.

Types of Adverbs

There are adverbs of frequency, manner, time, place and degree.
• Adverbs of frequency answer the question *How often?*.
We go to the doctor's for a check up **regularly**.
• Adverbs of manner answer the question *How?*.
She plays the piano so **beautifully**.
• Adverbs of time answer the question *When?*.
Sheila twisted her ankle **last week**.
• Adverbs of place answer the question *Where?*.
There is a medical centre **near** my block of flats.
• Adverbs of degree answer the question *To what extent?*.
It's **rather** cold today; I think I'll wear my jacket.

Order of Adverbs (Manner, Place & Time)

When we use two or more adverbs in a sentence, the usual order is **manner** + **place** + **time**.
She put the letter **carefully into her bag after leaving the post office**.
After verbs like *come, leave, go,* etc, the usual order is **place** + **manner** + **time**.
He walked to **the hospital quickly after** his meeting.

Time adverbs can also come at the beginning of a sentence.
After leaving the post office she put the letter carefully into her bag.
After his meeting he walked to the hospital quickly.

Order of Adverbs (Degree & Frequency)

Adverbs of degree such as *quite*, *rather*, *too* and *very* usually come before an adjective.
I am **quite good** at biology.
The book was **rather silly**.
They are **too young** to go to the park alone.
Her sister is a **very talented** surgeon.

Enough is also an adverb of degree, but it comes after an adjective or a verb.
The book wasn't **good enough** to win an award.
We **have enough** money to get two of these cakes.

Adverbs of frequency such as *always*, *never*, *seldom*, etc. usually come after the verb *be*, but before the main verb.
He **is always** home in the morning.
She **seldom washes** her hair before she goes to bed.

So & Such

We use *so* and *such* for emphasis. They are stronger than *very*.
• We use *so* + adjective/adverb.
This film is **so exciting**! I am really glad we came to see it!
• We use *such* + (adjective) + noun.
Your baby is **such a beautiful child**!

We can also use *so* and *such* to emphasise characteristics that lead to a certain result or action.
It was **such an exciting film** that I went to see it three times.
The band was **so bad** that we left the concert half way through.

Grammar Exercises

2 Look at the list of adjectives and write opinion (**OP**), colour (**C**), origin (**OR**), size (**S**) or material (**M**).

1 English _OR_   4 gorgeous _OP_   7 Italian _OR_   10 purple _C_   13 tiny _S_
2 French _OR_   5 horrible _OP_   8 lovely _OP_   11 red _C_   14 white _C_
3 glass _M_   6 huge _S_   9 metal _M_   12 small _S_   15 wooden _M_

3 Put the adjectives in the correct order.

1 a(n) English / huge / stone / country house
   a huge English stone country house

2 a(n) red / antique / round / tablecloth
   an antique round red tablecloth

3 a colourful / cool / big / balloon
   a cool big colourful balloon

4 Swiss / expensive / modern / watches
   expensive modern Swiss watches

5 a long / paperback / boring / French / novel
   a boring long French paperback novel

6 a chocolate / small / tasty / rabbit
   a tasty small chocolate rabbit

7 a(n) beautiful / woollen / orange / pullover
   a beautiful orange woollen pullover

8 a(n) Greek / interesting / ancient / myth
   an interesting ancient Greek myth

Unit 23

4 Complete the sentences with the correct -ed or -ing form of the words in brackets.

1 I'm not saying the lecture was ___boring___ (bore), but the speaker went on for too long.
2 Are you ___interested___ (interest) in sciences like biology and zoology?
3 I am so ___bored___ (bore) – I could scream!
4 The brain is an ___amazing___ (amaze) thing; perhaps one of the most complex things in the universe.
5 We like extreme sports, but they can be rather ___tiring___ (tire).
6 Sheila said that she had read a very ___interesting___ (interest) article about neurons yesterday.
7 The children are ___tired___ (tire) after playing in the park all day.
8 Hans was ___amazed___ (amaze) when he was told he had been accepted by Cambridge.

5 Rewrite the sentences. Sometimes more than one answer is possible.

1 Dad washes the car on Saturday. (always)
   Dad always washes the car on Saturday.
   On Saturday, Dad always washes the car.
2 I placed the crystal bowl. (on the shelf / gently)
   I placed the crystal bowl gently on the shelf.
3 We bought an expensive Irish linen tablecloth. (rather / last year / in Dublin)
   We bought a rather expensive Irish linen tablecloth in Dublin last year.
   Last year in Dublin we bought a rather expensive Irish linen tablecloth.
4 Jackie has been listening to music. (all morning / happily)
   Jackie has been happily listening to music all morning.
5 The doctor has been working. (all evening / in his surgery)
   The doctor has been working in his surgery all evening.
6 She left. (noisily / the classroom / during the lecture)
   She noisily left the classroom during the lecture.
   During the lecture she noisily left the classroom.
7 My sister cooks well. (usually / quite)
   My sister usually cooks quite well.
8 They were feeling happy. (extremely / after the match)
   They were feeling extremely happy after the match.
   After the match they were feeling extremely happy.

6 Complete the sentences with so, such, too or enough.

1 Billy is ___too___ young to know how to behave in fancy restaurants.
2 It was ___such___ a scary film that many people walked out.
3 My grades weren't good ___enough___ for me to get a scholarship.
4 This book is ___so___ interesting! I can't put it down!
5 I think I've got just ___enough___ money to take you to the cinema.
6 He's ___such___ a show off. Why does he act like that?
7 The food was ___so___ bad that I refused to pay for it.
8 Are you tall ___enough___ to reach that from the top shelf, Janet?

7 Choose the correct answers.

1 I got a ___ scarf for my birthday.
   a silk beautiful Italian
   b beautiful Italian silk
   c beautiful silk Italian

2 You look ___, Steven. Let's go out.
   a bored
   b bore
   c boring

3 Tony ___; I'm sure he'll win an award someday.
   a writes wonderful
   b writes wonderfully
   c wonderfully writes

4 Bob and Sue are ___ these days.
   a busy rather
   b rather busily
   c rather busy

5 I went ___.
   a to the dentist quickly after school
   b to the dentist after school quickly
   c after school to the dentist quickly

6 His uncle is a ___ brain surgeon.
   a very famous
   b very famously
   c famous very

7 He ___ to be able to bake a cake.
   a enough knows
   b knows enough
   c knowingly enough

8 It was ___ that I wanted to learn more.
   a too a fascinating subject
   b so a fascinating subject
   c such a fascinating subject

Vocabulary

Phrasal verbs

8 Complete the table with these prepositions to form phrasal verbs. You will have to use some of the prepositions more than once.

away   for   in   off   out   out of   over   up

back	(1) _away_	(2) _out of_
hand	(3) _out_	(4) _over_
head	(5) _out_	(6) _for_
run	(7) _out of_	(8) _over_
think	(9) _up_	(10) _over_
stand	(11) _out_	(12) _in_

9 Complete the sets of sentences with the correct form of the phrasal verbs from 8.

1 a If you come across an angry dog, _back away_ from it slowly.
  b You can't _back out of_ our deal; we shook hands on it!

2 a Can you help me _think up_ some ways to plan the party without Mum knowing about it?
  b You don't have to agree to it now. _Think_ it _over_ and I'll email you tomorrow.

3 a Where is John going? It looks like he's _heading for_ the park.
  b Well, I think we'd better _head out_ now or we'll be late for the meeting.

4 a The race was nearly over and many of the runners had _run out of_ breath.
  b Don't ride your bike in the road! You'll get _run over_ by a car.

5 a She had gorgeous long blonde hair which really made her _stand out_ in a crowd.
  b Our biology teacher was off sick, so the PE teacher had to _stand in_ for her.

6 a Stop right there, thief! _Hand over_ the stolen money or we'll shoot!
  b There's a man on the corner _handing out_ leaflets for the new museum.

Unit 23

Exam Practice

Word formation

10 Use the word in capitals to form a word that fits in the gap.

1. Joey can't write with his right hand because he's ___left-handed___. — **HAND**
2. Kay sews ___beautifully___; you should get her to make your wedding dress. — **BEAUTIFUL**
3. Dad! Come ___quickly___. Our dog is chasing the neighbour's cat! — **QUICK**
4. The woman had had a hard life, so she had many lines on her ___forehead___. — **HEAD**
5. Did you know that some lizards have no ___eyelids___? They can't blink! — **LID**
6. I can't watch ___frightening___ films – they give me nightmares. — **FRIGHTEN**
7. This is cool. A person normally ___breathes___ 23,000 times a day! — **BREATH**
8. I read a book about the human body and I must say that I'm ___amazed___! — **AMAZE**

Cloze

11 Choose the correct answers.

1. Listen to this – humans are the only animal that have a ___.
   - **(a) thumb** b stomach c thigh
2. In pictures, Santa Claus usually has a lovely long white ___.
   - a hair **(b) beard** c face
3. Pat fell and twisted her ___ while playing soccer.
   - a calf **(b) ankle** c chest
4. If you spill salt, throw a little over your ___ for good luck.
   - a hip b elbow **(c) shoulder**
5. Why are you ___ your eye like that? Did you get something in it?
   - a crying b laughing **(c) blinking**
6. Grandpa is going to the doctor's tonight to have his ___ pressure checked.
   - a water **(b) blood** c sweat
7. The weight-lifter's arm ___ were so large that he could only wear sleeveless shirts.
   - a cells **(b) muscles** c bones
8. Ouch! I was eating a biscuit and I bit my ___.
   - a cheek b neck **(c) tongue**

What Do You Think?

Speaking

12 Talk to your partner about the following:

- how often he/she goes to the dentist.
- when the last time was that he/she went to the doctor.
- what his/her favourite item of clothing is like.
- what the house/flat he/she lives in is like.
- how well he/she can cook/sing/dance.

Unit 24

Awareness

1 Which of these sentences are correct (C) and incorrect (I)?

1. Jason has big muscles than me. — _I_
2. My father is intelligent than your father. — _I_
3. Have elephants got larger brains than humans? — _C_
4. Can your classmates run faster than you? — _C_
5. The cheetah is the quickest animal on the planet. — _C_
6. That was most interesting lecture I've ever been to. — _I_
7. Wow! This is the tidiest I've ever seen your bedroom! — _C_
8. Tony writes good, but his reading needs some work. — _I_
9. Snakes are my mother's least favourite animal – they scare her. — _C_
10. He's not nice as his cousin. — _I_

How many did you get right? ☐

Grammar
Comparison of Adjectives & Adverbs

We use the comparative to compare two people or things. We usually form the comparative by adding *-er* to an adjective or adverb. If the adjective or adverb has two or more syllables, we use the word *more*. We often use the word *than* after the comparative.
Betty has got **shorter** hair **than** Pam.
This silver MP3 player is **more expensive than** the black one.

We use the superlative to compare one person or thing with other people or things of the same type. We usually form the superlative by adding *-est* to the adjective or adverb. If the adjective or adverb has two or more syllables, we usually use the word *most*. We use the word *the* before the superlative.
That was **the best** meal I've ever had.
She is **the most interesting** person we have ever met.

Spelling: big ➔ bi**gger**/bi**ggest**, nice ➔ nic**er**/nic**est**, tidy ➔ tid**ier**/tid**iest**

Some adjectives and adverbs are irregular and form their comparative and superlative in different ways.

Adjective/Adverb	Comparative	Superlative
good/well	better	the best
bad/badly	worse	the worst
many	more	the most
much	more	the most
little	less	the least
far	farther/further	the farthest/furthest

Unit 24

Other Comparative Structures

We use *as* + adjective/adverb + *as* to show that two people or things are similar in some way.
My bike is **as fast as** your bike.
We use *not as/so ... as* to show that one person or thing has less of a quality than another.
I am **not as handsome as** my brother is.

Grammar Exercises

2 Complete the table.

Adjective/Adverb	Comparative	Superlative
tasty	(1) tastier	(2) the tastiest
exciting	(3) more exciting	(4) the most exciting
carefully	(5) more carefully	(6) the most carefully
bad/badly	(7) worse	(8) the worst
little	(9) less	(10) the least
tidy	(11) tidier	(12) the tidiest
late	(13) later	(14) the latest
sad	(15) sadder	(16) the saddest
far	(17) farther / further	(18) the farthest / the furthest
beautifully	(19) more beautifully	(20) the most beautifully

3 Complete the sentences with the correct form of the adjectives and adverbs from the table in 2.

1 Why is your sister's room _____tidier_____ than yours? Yours is a complete mess!
2 Is a litre of milk _____less_____ than a cup of milk?
3 It's four in the morning! This is _____the latest_____ I've ever stayed up in my life!
4 Dad is _____the most careful_____ driver I know. He has never had an accident.
5 My house is _____farther/further_____ than yours from the school.
6 Scientists say that this winter is going to be _____worse_____ than last winter. I'd better get out my warmest clothes!
7 That was _____the tastiest_____ pizza I've ever eaten – you must give me your recipe.
8 If you asked me, I'd say that bungee jumping is _____more exciting_____ than parachuting. They're both thrilling though!
9 Look at these two paintings. Do you think Julia paints _____more beautifully_____ than me, or is mine nicer?
10 That was _____the saddest_____ story I've ever heard; I've still got tears in my eyes.

4 Circle the correct words.

1 Hans runs most quickly /(more quickly) than Doug – I think he'll win the race.
2 Doris is not nice – she's less /(the least) liked girl in the school.
3 Which planet is (the farthest)/ farther planet from the sun?
4 Clive is the younger /(the youngest) child in his family.
5 Tommy is more clever /(more clever than) Steven.
6 I think this is the more interesting /(the most interesting) article I've read.
7 Fran is gooder /(better) at maths than me, but she's (worse)/ badder than me at biology.
8 That is (the dirtiest)/ the most dirtiest kitchen I've ever seen; let's go to a different restaurant!
9 I have much /(more) time to have fun in the summer than in the winter.
10 All the boys in the class study, but George studies (the hardest)/ the harder.

5 Choose the correct answers.

1 This box is ___ than that one.
   a the heavier
   b the heaviest
   (c) heavier than

2 Little Karen sang ___ of all the children in the choir.
   a the more happier
   (b) the most happily
   c the most happily than

3 Look! That is ___ puppy I've ever seen!
   (a) the fattest
   b the fatest
   c the fatter

4 My mother is ___ your mother.
   a so pretty as
   (b) as pretty as
   c as pretty so

5 This state-of-the-art microscope is ___ that older model.
   a the most expensive than
   (b) more expensive than
   c the more expensive than

6 They both work busily, but Clem works ___ than Joe.
   (a) more busily
   b most busily
   c the more busily

7 Canada is ___ from Australia than it is from the USA.
   a the furthest
   (b) farther
   c farthest

8 Joey isn't ___ his big brother.
   a as intelligent so
   b as intelligent than
   (c) so intelligent as

6 Complete the sentences with the correct comparative or superlative form of the words in brackets. Add words where necessary.

1 That was _____*the most delicious*_____ (delicious) cake ever – I couldn't eat another bite!
2 Dean solves difficult problems _____*more easily than*_____ (easily) I do.
3 Your dog, Leo, is _____*the most gentle*_____ (gentle) animal I've ever seen.
4 Nobody does their homework _____*more carefully than*_____ (carefully) Joe does.
5 I've been learning the guitar for a year now, so I'm _____*better than*_____ (good) I was last year.
6 I bought a new telescope – it was _____*the cheapest*_____ (cheap) one in the shop.
7 Stella draws badly, but I draw _____*worse than*_____ (bad) her.
8 I think that ballet is _____*the most creative*_____ (creative) of all the performing arts.

7 Complete the sentences with your opinions and the correct comparative or superlative form of the words in brackets. Add words where necessary. *Students' own answers but for the adjectives and adverbs as follows:*

1 When it comes to sports, I don't think _____*skiing*_____ is so _____*challenging as*_____ (challenging) hockey.
2 As far as I'm concerned, _____ is _____*the loveliest*_____ (lovely) place I've ever visited.
3 I think that the _____ is _____*the scariest*_____ (scary) animal of all.
4 As far as school subjects go, I feel that _____ is _____*as difficult*_____ (difficult) as _____.
5 _____ is _____*the friendliest*_____ (friendly) person I've ever met.
6 Let's talk about actors – I think _____ acts _____*better*_____ (good) than _____.
7 In my opinion, _____ is as _____*successful as*_____ (successful) yours.

Unit 24

Vocabulary

Word formation

8 Complete the table.

noun	verb	adjective	adverb
(1) _beautician_ / beauty	beautify	beautiful	beautifully
energy	energise	(2) _energetic_	energetically
(3) _height_	heighten	high	highly
(4) _information_	inform	informative	informatively
length	(5) _lengthen_	long	–
memory	memorise	(6) _memorable_	memorably
strength	strengthen	strong	(7) _strongly_
(8) _width_	widen	wide	widely

9 Complete the sentences with words from the table in 8.

1 It's been a(n) _____long_____ difficult day and I'm tired; I think I'll go to bed.
2 If you want to _____beautify_____ your house or flat, call *Interior Design Inc.* today!
3 In his article, the scientist wrote _____informatively_____ about how certain foods affect the human body.
4 That shelf is up too _____high_____ for Johnny to reach.
5 I really need to get in shape, but, to tell the truth, I just don't have the _____energy_____.
6 I have to _____memorise_____ the Latin names of all these plants for biology class – I'll be here for ages!
7 We really have to _____widen_____ this door; it's too narrow for Big John to get through!
8 Don't you think that this soup smells _____strongly_____ of garlic?

Exam Practice

Cloze

10 Choose the correct answers.

1 Is your house ___ away from the gym than mine?
   a farthest   b far   **c farther**
2 He's got ___ money than you – you pay for the meal!
   a little   b least   **c less**
3 Joe is a very ___ person; I think that's why he has done so well for himself.
   a confident b shy   c thin
4 I'm not keen on people that are ___ losers; they should be more sportsman-like.
   a bad   b worst   c badly
5 Hello. I'm looking for the ___ expensive lab equipment in the shop.
   a more   **b most**   c much
6 Jake is more ___ than Jason because he works much harder.
   a successfully **b successful** c success
7 Pat has got an amazing ___; she's fun and really energetic.
   a eyebrow   b feature   **c personality**
8 Chris fits in more ___ with the other children than Lyle does.
   a easily   b easy   c easiest

Sentence transformation

11 Complete the second sentence so that it has a similar meaning to the first sentence, using the word given. Do not change the word given. You must use between two and five words.

1. Hans is fatter than Grant.
   so
   Grant is not _____ *so fat as* _____ Hans.

2. We've never seen such an amazing sight.
   the
   It's _____ *the most amazing* _____ sight we've ever seen.

3. Professor Jenkins and Professor Jones speak well, but Professor Colins speaks even better.
   best
   Professor Colins _____ *speaks best* _____ of all.

4. Trent is more imaginative than Sheila.
   as
   Sheila _____ *isn't as imaginative* _____ as Trent.

5. Mum is 35 years old and Dad is 40 years old.
   than
   Dad _____ *is older than* _____ Mum.

6. She works hard to be successful. Her brother doesn't try hard enough.
   harder
   She _____ *works harder than* _____ her brother to be successful.

7. This glass is a quarter full of water. This bottle is half full of water. This vase is full of water.
   the
   The glass has got _____ *the least* _____ water of all.

8. Today's weather isn't as nice as yesterday's.
   worse
   The weather is _____ *worse today than it was* _____ yesterday.

What Do You Think?

Writing

12 Read the writing task below and write the letter in your notebook. Make sure your letter has an introduction (Paragraph 1), a main body (Paragraphs 2 and 3) and a conclusion (Paragraph 4).

Karen, one of your cousins, recently sent you a letter about a new gym that has opened in your area that she wants to join. She thinks you might want to join too because she knows you like to keep fit. Write a letter to Karen asking her about the gym's opening hours, how much it costs to join and what facilities the gym has on offer.

Review 6

Grammar

1 Rewrite the sentences using the causative.

1 Someone had installed storm windows at the cottage for them.
   They had had storm windows installed at the cottage.
2 Ms Blanche must make the team's uniforms by the end of the month.
   The team must have their uniforms made by Ms Blanche by the end of the month.
3 A carpenter is going to make some book shelves for me.
   I'm going to have some book shelves made for me by a carpenter.
4 Gale's uncle will fix her leaking tap for her.
   Gale will have her leaking tap fixed for her by her uncle.
5 New computers were delivered to Dad's office.
   Dad's office had new computers delivered.
6 Billy's skateboard was stolen at the park.
   Billy had his skateboard stolen at the park.
7 Are they planting a garden outside the school?
   Are they having a garden planted outside the school?
8 Someone walks the Smiths' dog every day.
   The Smiths have their dog walked every day.

2 Complete the sentences with the -ing or the correct form of the infinitive of the verbs in brackets.

1 Teachers expect students ___*to hand in*___ (hand in) their assignments on time.
2 Would you enjoy ___*attending*___ (attend) a camp where you would learn about nature and the environment?
3 You could ___*become*___ (become) fitter by eating properly and getting lots of exercise.
4 How much time do most students spend ___*surfing*___ (surf) the Internet each week?
5 Timothy, would you like ___*to come*___ (come) to the end-of-term party with me?
6 They'd better ___*try*___ (try) harder than that if they want to graduate this year.
7 Special equipment, telescopes and microscopes for example, can be used ___*to help*___ (help) us better understand our world.
8 Young children learn how to behave by ___*following*___ (follow) the examples of others.
9 At Northumberland Secondary School we aim ___*to educate*___ (educate) children, so they become responsible adults.
10 It's rather hard to believe, but I'm not sure that my son understands the importance of ___*studying*___ (study) for tests.

3 Choose the correct answers.

1 That was an ___ video; I wish they'd produce more like that.
   a exciting
   b excited
2 It was ___ that I wanted to stay there forever.
   a such a nice island
   b so a nice island
3 Doesn't Ms Jackson ___? I love that dress.
   a beautifully dress
   b dress beautifully
4 The teacher walked ___.
   a to the parking lot after classes were over
   b after classes were over to the parking lot
5 It's ___ today; I think I'll open the windows.
   a rather warm
   b rather warmly
6 There was a ___ fence around my grandmother's little cottage.
   a white wooden lovely
   b lovely white wooden
7 Professor Jenkins is a ___ writer and lecturer.
   a very intelligently
   b very intelligent
8 Jake is ___ to get that down for you; Ask him.
   a enough tall
   b tall enough

4 Complete the sentences with the correct comparative or superlative form of the words in brackets. Add words where necessary.

1. He's got _____more_____ (many) books than anyone else I know.
2. Ms Patten works _____harder_____ (hard) than Mr Jones; they're both good teachers though.
3. My sister gets good grades _____more easily_____ (easily) than I do.
4. You're _____the best_____ (good) cook I know; why don't you make me dinner?
5. Mum got me a new desk for my birthday; it was _____the biggest_____ (big) one in the shop.
6. Is the secondary school _____farther/further_____ (far) away from Elm Street than the primary school?
7. Biology is _____the most interesting_____ (interesting) subject on the school curriculum.
8. Brett Hines thinks _____the most imaginatively_____ (imaginatively) of all the candidates – let's hire him.

5 Find the mistakes and correct the sentences where necessary. Put a tick (✓) below those which do not need correcting.

1. Do you think that your schedule is as busier as mine?
   Do you think that your schedule is as busy as mine?
2. My new boyfriend drives an expensive modern black convertible.
   ✓
3. In my opinion, last year's holiday wasn't so memorable so this year's.
   In my opinion, last year's holiday wasn't so memorable as this year's.
4. My grandfather can't hear as good as my grandmother, but he can see good than her.
   My grandfather can't hear as well as my grandmother, but he can see better than her.
5. I'm afraid the head teacher is too busy speaking with you right now.
   I'm afraid the head teacher is too busy to speak with you right now.
6. The children stopped seeing the little puppy in the pet shop window.
   The children stopped to see the little puppy in the pet shop window.
7. My brother is interested in to become a brain surgeon.
   My brother is interested in becoming a brain surgeon.
8. They usually meet after class regularly for a coffee.
   They usually meet regularly after class for a coffee.
9. My mum is going to dye her hair tomorrow by a famous stylist.
   My mum is going to have her hair dyed tomorrow by a famous stylist.
10. Will that artist have his sculptures exhibited at the gallery next month?
    ✓

Review 6

6 Circle the correct words.
1. This is a very bored / **boring** programme; I think I'll go to bed.
2. Looking after your body is such / **so** important.
3. It was **such** / very a gorgeous day that I decided to take the day off work!
4. Joe will check his eyes / **will have his eyes checked** at the optician's today.
5. We're having a garden planted for / **by** professionals.
6. Oh no! I forgot **to bring** / bringing my maths book home from school!
7. Just a reminder. Students must to hand in / **hand in** their projects by tomorrow.
8. We went to the gym **to use** / using the exercise equipment.
9. The baby wakes up **later** / the latest than the rest of the children.
10. Hans speaks **the most quietly** / the more quiet of all the boys in the class.

Use of English
Open cloze

7 Complete the sentences with the word that best fits each gap.
1. I was very glad ____to____ hear that you got into university.
2. We've ____run____ out of milk; I'll go to the shop and get some.
3. Nancy ____had____ her leg broken while skiing yesterday.
4. We're having the computer installed ____by____ the technician now.
5. There's our maths teacher. I wonder where he's heading ____for____.
6. ____Are____ they having new carpets laid in their living room?
7. My mum complains ____more____ than other mums – I'm sure of it!
8. I know you can do it. All you have to do is ____make____ an effort.
9. That was ____the____ most difficult exam I've ever written.
10. Joan can write ____as____ well as her twin sister, Jane.

Word formation

8 Use the word in capitals to form a word that fits in the gap.
1. Once he finishes ____secondary____ school, he's planning to go to university. **SECOND**
2. That lecture was so ____informative____ that I'm really glad that I went. **INFORM**
3. If you have the right ____qualifications____, you may get the job. **QUALIFY**
4. Is it true that fish ____breathe____ through their gills? Or is that a myth? **BREATH**
5. Can you believe that Ms Dean gave us a(n) ____assignment____? It's the holidays! **ASSIGN**
6. We really need to ____strengthen____ this step or someone is going to fall through it. **STRONG**
7. Juanita's ____pronunciation____ is rather odd, but she has an incredible vocabulary. **PRONOUNCE**
8. Sheila may not be gorgeous, but she has got a great ____personality____. **PERSON**

Grammar

9 For questions 1–10, choose the word or phrase that best completes the sentence.

1. Is Joel ___ to join the school swimming team?
   A very good
   B good enough
   C too good

2. ___ by a babysitter during the day?
   A Do her children look after
   B Does she have her children looked after
   C Are her children look after

3. The candidates ___ by Ms Simms.
   A will get their applications collect
   B will collect their applications
   C will have their applications collected

4. ___ is the best pastime in the world.
   A Ski
   B To ski
   C Skiing

5. Poor George ___ at the gym today.
   A is having his phone stolen
   B got his phone stolen
   C had stolen his phone

6. Liz ___; it's part of her job.
   A always goes to the lab on weekday afternoons
   B goes always to the lab on weekday afternoons
   C on weekday afternoons goes always to the lab

7. It's getting cold outside; you'd better ___ a pullover.
   A to wear
   B wear
   C wearing

8. Feta is a ___ cheese that is very good for you.
   A white tasty Greek
   B Greek tasty white
   C tasty white Greek

9. I'm afraid I can't afford ___ you anywhere nice for your graduation dinner.
   A to take
   B take
   C taking

10. That was ___ soup I've ever had – it was far too salty.
    A the worse
    B baddest
    C the worst

Vocabulary

10 For questions 11–20, choose the word or phrase that best completes the sentence.

11. Which of the ___ did you think was the most qualified for the position?
    A candidates
    B accents
    C subjects

12. Tony, could you help me ___ out the test papers, please?
    A head
    B back
    C hand

13. If you ___ too many lessons in one term, you'll be expelled.
    A pass
    B miss
    C lose

14. Her long dyed purple hair really makes her ___ out in a crowd, doesn't it?
    A think
    B stand
    C run

15. Have you noticed there has been an increase ___ the number of students coming late to class?
    A in
    B of
    C at

16. If I want to go to university, I need to get a ___.
    A graduation
    B scholarship
    C curriculum

17. Mum and Dad are very satisfied ___ the grades I got this year.
    A from
    B about
    C with

18. Older people should have their ___ pressure checked regularly.
    A sweat
    B blood
    C water

19. That man has got the longest and whitest ___ I've ever seen!
    A eyelids
    B eyebrows
    C eyes

20. Once you ___ a taste for jogging, you'll want to do it every morning.
    A get
    B make
    C break

Irregular verbs

Infinitive	Past Simple	Past Participle
be	was/were	been
beat	beat	beaten
become	became	become
begin	began	begun
bite	bit	bitten
blow	blew	blown
break	broke	broken
bring	brought	brought
broadcast	broadcast	broadcast
build	built	built
burn	burnt	burnt
buy	bought	bought
can	could	–
catch	caught	caught
choose	chose	chosen
come	came	come
cost	cost	cost
cut	cut	cut
deal	dealt	dealt
dig	dug	dug
do	did	done
draw	drew	drawn
dream	dreamt	dreamt
drink	drank	drunk
drive	drove	driven
eat	ate	eaten
fall	fell	fallen
feed	fed	fed
feel	felt	felt
fight	fought	fought
find	found	found
fly	flew	flown
forecast	forecast	forecast
forget	forgot	forgotten
get	got	got
give	gave	given
go	went	gone
grow	grew	grown
have	had	had
hear	heard	heard
hide	hid	hidden
hit	hit	hit
hold	held	held
hurt	hurt	hurt
keep	kept	kept
know	knew	known
lead	led	led
learn	learnt	learnt
leave	left	left
lend	lent	lent
let	let	let
lie	lay	lain

Infinitive	Past Simple	Past Participle
light	lit	lit
lose	lost	lost
mean	meant	meant
make	made	made
meet	met	met
pay	paid	paid
prove	proved	proven
put	put	put
read	read[red]	read[red]
ride	rode	ridden
ring	rang	rung
rise	rose	risen
run	ran	run
say	said	said
see	saw	seen
sell	sold	sold
send	sent	sent
set	set	set
shake	shook	shaken
shine	shone	shone
show	showed	shown
shoot	shot	shot
shut	shut	shut
sing	sang	sung
sink	sank	sunk
sit	sat	sat
sleep	slept	slept
slide	slid	slid
smell	smelt	smelt
speak	spoke	spoken
speed	sped	sped
spend	spent	spent
stand	stood	stood
steal	stole	stolen
stick	stuck	stuck
stink	stank	stunk
sweep	swept	swept
swim	swam	swum
take	took	taken
teach	taught	taught
tell	told	told
think	thought	thought
throw	threw	thrown
understand	understood	understood
wake	woke	woken
wear	wore	worn
win	won	won
write	wrote	written
wear	wore	worn
win	won	won
write	wrote	written

Phrasal verbs

act out	=	perform	(U19)
ask someone out	=	to invite someone to go out with you	(U8)
back away	=	to move away backwards	(U23)
back out of	=	to decide you are no longer taking part in something that has been agreed	(U23)
break off	=	to turn bad	(U3)
call for	=	to require	(U16)
call of	=	to cancel	(U11)
call out	=	to announce	(U16)
catch on	=	become popular	(U19)
cheer (someone) on	=	to encourage them loudly	(U11)
chop up	=	to cut into pieces	(U3)
come across	=	to find something	(U3)
come down	=	to fall	(U3)
cool off	=	to calm down	(U11)
cut down	=	to reduce	(U3)
cut out for	=	to be suited to	(U16)
eat out	=	to go to a restaurant	(U3)
end up	=	to finish	(U11)
find out	=	to discover	(U16)
get on	=	to have a good relationship with	(U8)
get something down	=	write something down	(U19)
give out	=	distribute	(U19)
go down	=	to be remembered as	(U11)
go off	=	to stop doing something	(U3)
grow apart	=	to stop having a close relationship with someone	(U8)
grow out of	=	be too old for something	(U19)
hand out	=	to give a number of things to people in a group	(U23)
hand over	=	to give something to another person	(U23)
hang out	=	to spend time with someone socially	(U8)
head for	=	to move in a particular direction	(U23)
head out	=	to leave	(U23)
hold back	=	to stop yourself from expressing how you really feel	(U8)
kick off	=	to start	(U11)
let (someone) down	=	to fail to help or support someone as they hoped or expected	(U8)
look up to (someone)	=	to admire and respect	(U8)
make up	=	to become friends again with someone	(U8)
peel off	=	to remove the skin or outer covering from a fruit or a vegetable	(U3)
put (someone) down	=	to make somebody look or feel stupid	(U8)
run out of	=	to use up or finish a supply	(U23)
run over	=	to knock a person or an animal down and drive over their body	(U23)
sell out	=	run out of something	(U19)
show off	=	to behave boastfully	(U16)
stand in	=	to take someone's place	(U23)
stand out	=	to be noticeable	(U23)
stick up for (someone)	=	to support or defend someone	(U8)
take in	=	to make something smaller	(U3)
take out	=	to remove from somewhere or something	(U3)
take to	=	to start to like	(U16)
take up	=	to begin	(U16)
think over	=	to consider something carefully before reaching a decision	(U23)
think up	=	to create something in your mind	(U23)

try out for	=	to audition	(U16)
turn away	=	refuse somebody admission	(U19)
turn on	=	switch on	(U19)
turn out	=	end in a particular way	(U19)
turn up	=	increase the volume	(U19)
warm up	=	to prepare your body	(U11)
wear out	=	to get old and damaged	(U11)

Prepositions

(be) a good case **in** point	(U9)	large amounts **of** something	(U22)
(be) a statement **about** something	(U9)	lead **to** something	(U17)
(be) prepared **for** something	(U9)	look **for** answers	(U17)
a place **at** university	(U22)	make their way **onto** something	(U5)
about the same size	(U13)	not be the case **at** all	(U9)
above sea level	(U13)	**on** the planet	(U13)
after a few minutes of doing something	(U9)	**over** 32 degrees Celsius	(U13)
after years of something	(U5)	**over** the years	(U13)
an increase **in** something	(U22)	pin money **to**	(U2)
at a certain age	(U22)	raise awareness **about** something	(U5)
at the end **of**	(U2)	rely **on** something/somebody	(U17)
at the moment	(U5)	show up **in** something	(U5)
be an expert **on** something	(U17)	something **of** the house	(U9)
be successful **in** doing something	(U17)	stretch from somewhere **to** somewhere else	(U5)
before something happens	(U5)	stretched **across**	(U13)
below freezing	(U13)	take a look **at**	(U2)
come **under** threat	(U17)	take a look **at** somebody/something	(U9)
communicate **with** somebody	(U17)	the top **of** the mountain	(U13)
compare somebody/something **to** somebody/something else	(U9)	throw a little **over** your shoulder	(U2)
concerned **about** something	(U17)	to apply **for** something	(U22)
covered **from** head to toe	(U2)	to be bad **at** something	(U22)
decorates it **with** pretty ribbons	(U2)	to be good **at** something	(U22)
everything **from** something to something else	(U5)	to be satisfied **with** something	(U22)
for a reason	(U9)	to concentrate **on** something	(U22)
for good luck	(U2)	to spend money **on** something	(U22)
for **over** twenty years	(U5)	to suffer **from** something	(U22)
friends **of** mine	(U2)	to worry **about** something	(U22)
go **on** safari	(U17)	turn **into** something	(U5)
in a desert	(U13)	use something instead **of** something else	(U17)
in countries	(U2)	walk slowly **through**	(U2)
in the water	(U13)	**within** a reason	(U9)

Collocations & Expressions

(be) a bookworm	(U21)	have sympathy	(U1)
(be) in the teacher's good books	(U21)	keep a diary	(U1)
(be) on the verge of	(U6)	keep a secret	(U1)
a buyer's market	(U18)	keep calm	(U14)
are selling like hotcakes	(U18)	leads the field	(U18)
break the rules	(U21)	made-to-order	(U18)
bring attention to	(U6)	make a journey	(U14)
burn the candle at both ends	(U21)	make a mess	(U10)
buy (something) off the peg	(U18)	make an effort	(U21)
do (your) best	(U14)	make payments	(U10)
do research	(U6)	make progress	(U21)
do the dishes	(U10)	make your bed	(U10)
do the housework	(U10)	mass production	(U18)
face great danger	(U6)	move house	(U10)
fall in love	(U1)	move mountains	(U10)
fall to pieces	(U1)	move with the times	(U10)
fight pollution	(U6)	pay a compliment	(U1)
form a group	(U6)	pay a visit	(U1)
get a taste for (something)	(U21)	save (someone's) life	(U14)
get divorced	(U1)	save energy	(U6)
get lost	(U14)	see results	(U14)
get married	(U1)	state of the art	(U18)
get the hang of (something)	(U21)	take a bath	(U10)
go missing	(U14)	take a break	(U10)
have a family	(U1)	take action	(U6)
have a narrow escape	(U14)	top of the range	(U18)

Word formation

Adjective → Adjective		
ELDER	ELDERLY	U1
SECOND	SECONDARY	U22

Adjective → Noun		
STRANGE	STRANGER	U8
WEAK	WEAKNESS	R3

Adverbs		
ACT	ACTIVELY	U20
BEAUTIFUL	BEAUTIFULLY	U23
BRIGHT	BRIGHTLY	U4
COMPETITIVE	COMPETITIVELY	U12
CREATE	CREATIVELY	U20
DANGEROUS	DANGEROUSLY	U12
DEEP	DEEPLY	U12
DEFINED	DEFINITELY	U12
DRAMATISE	DRAMATICALLY	U20
ENERGETIC	ENERGETICALLY	U24
FREE	FREELY	U12
HIGH	HIGHLY	U24
IMAGINE	IMAGINATIVELY	U20
INFORMATIVE	INFORMATIVELY	U24
MEMORABLE	MEMORABLY	U24
MYSTIFY	MYSTERIOUSLY	U20
PRODUCE	PRODUCTIVELY	U20
PROPER	PROPERLY	U12
QUICK	QUICKLY	U23
STRONG	STRONGLY	U24
WIDE	WIDELY	U24

Noun → Adjective		
ARROGANCE	ARROGANT	U1
BEAUTICIAN/ BEAUTY	BEAUTIFUL	U24
CHOICE	CHOOSY	U4
COLOUR	COLOURED/COLOURFUL	U4
COURAGE	COURAGEOUS	U8
CUSTOM/ CUSTOMER	CUSTOMARY	U4
DECISION	DECISIVE	U4
ENERGY	ENERGETIC	U24
GLOBE	GLOBAL	U5
HAND	LEFT-HANDED	U23
HEIGHT	HIGH	U24
HUNGER	HUNGRY	U3
INFORMATION	INFORMATIVE	U24
LENGTH	LONG	U24
MEMORY	MEMORABLE	U24
MIXTURE	MIXED/MIXING	U4
NATURE	NATURAL	U5
NUTRITION	NUTRITIOUS	U3
ORGAN	ORGANIC	U5
PERSON	PERSONAL	U8
REASON	REASONABLE	U1
RELATION	RELATIONSHIP	U8
STRENGTH	STRONG	U24
TASTE	TASTY/TASTEFUL/TASTELESS	U4
TRADITION	TRADITIONAL	U4
TREND	TRENDY	U4
VARIETY	VARIOUS	U4
WIDTH	WIDE	U24

Noun → Verb		
ACTOR/ACTING	ACT	U20
ASSISTANT/ASSISTANCE	ASSIST	U12
BEAUTICIAN/BEAUTY	BEAUTIFY	U24
BREATH	BREATHE	U23
BRIGHT	BRIGHTEN	U4
CHOICE	CHOOSE	U4
COLOUR	COLOUR	U4
COMPETITION/COMPETITOR	COMPETE	U12
CONCENTRATION	CONCENTRATE	U12
CREATOR/CREATION	CREATE	U20
DANGER	ENDANGER	U12
DECISION	DECIDE	U4
DEFINITION	DEFINE	U12
DEPTH	DEEPEN	U12
DRAMA	DRAMATISE	U20
ENERGY	ENERGISE	U24
ENTERTAINMENT/ENTERTAINER	ENTERTAIN	U20
FOLLOWER	FOLLOW	U12
FREEDOM	FREE	U12
GRIEF	GRIEVE	U1
HEIGHT	HEIGHTEN	U24
IMAGINATION	IMAGINE	U20
INFORMATION	INFORM	U24
LENGTH	LENGTHEN	U24
MEMORY	MEMORISE	U24
MIXTURE	MIX	U4
MYSTERY	MYSTIFY	U20
PERFORMER/PERFORMANCE	PERFORM	U20
PRODUCER/PRODUCTION	PRODUCE	U20
REVOLUTION	REVOLUTIONISE	R5
STRENGTH	STRENGTHEN	U24
SUPERVISOR/SUPERVISION	SUPERVISE	U12
TASTE	TASTE	U4
VARIETY	VARY	U4
WIDTH	WIDEN	U24

Noun → Noun		
ATHLETE	ATHLETICS	R3
CHAMPION	CHAMPIONSHIP	R3
EXAM	EXAMINER	U22
GENE	GENETICS	U1
HEAD	FOREHEAD	U23
LID	EYELID	U23
PHOTO	PHOTOGRAPHY	R4
QUALITY	QUALIFICATION	U22
SCHOLAR	SCHOLARSHIP	U22

Prefixes		
APPEAR	DISAPPEARED	R4
COME	OVERCOME	R4
DANGER	ENDANGERED	U5
RECOGNISE	UNRECOGNISABLE	U16

Word formation

Verb → Adjective		
AMAZE	AMAZED	U23
APPRECIATE	APPRECIATIVE	U8
ARGUE	ARGUMENTATIVE	U7
ASSIST	ASSISTANT	U12
BENEFIT	BENEFICIAL	R2
BOIL	BOILING	U3
BORE	BORING	U7
COMMUNICATE	COMMUNICATIVE	U7
COMPETE	COMPETITIVE	U12
CONCENTRATE	CONCENTRATED	U12
CONGRATULATE	CONGRATULATORY	U15
DEEPEN	DEEP	U12
DEFINE	DEFINED	U12
EDUCATE	EDUCATIONAL	U16
EMBARRASS	EMBARRASSED	U7
ENDANGER	DANGEROUS	U12
ENGAGE	ENGAGED	U7
ENTERTAIN	ENTERTAINING	U16
ENTHUSE	ENTHUSIASTIC	R5
FOLLOW	FOLLOWING	U12
FREE	FREE	U12
FRIGHTEN	FRIGHTENING	U23
IMPRESS	IMPRESSIVE	U15
IRRITATE	IRRITATED	U8
MARRY	MARRIED	U7
OBEY	OBEDIENT	R2
OBSERVE	OBSERVANT	U15
PLEASE	PLEASANT	U7
RELY	RELIABLE	U1
RENEW	RENEWABLE	U5
SAVOUR	SAVOURY	U3
SUPERVISE	SUPERVISED	U12
SUPPORT	SUPPORTIVE	U15
SUSPECT	SUSPICIOUS	R2
SYMPATHISE	SYMPATHETIC	U7
TASTE	TASTELESS	U4

Verb → Noun		
ACQUAINT	ACQUAINTANCE	U8
ARGUE	ARGUMENT	U7
ASSIGN	ASSIGNMENT	U22
BORE	BOREDOM	U7
CELEBRATE	CELEBRITY/CELEBRATION	U15
COLLECT	COLLECTION	U16
COMMUNICATE	COMMUNICATION	U7
CONGRATULATE	CONGRATULATIONS	U15
CONSERVE	CONSERVATION	U5
COOK	COOKER	U3
COOK	COOKERY	R4
DESTROY	DESTRUCTION	U5
EMBARRASS	EMBARRASSMENT	U7
ENGAGE	ENGAGEMENT	U7
ENROL	ENROLMENT	U22
EXTEND	EXTENSION	R3
EXTINCT	EXTINCTION	U5
FASCINATE	FASCINATION	U16
GRADUATE	GRADUATION	U22
ILLUSTRATE	ILLUSTRATION	U16
IMPRESS	IMPRESSION	U15
INFORM	INFORMATION	R5
MARRY	MARRIAGE	U1, U7
NAVIGATE	NAVIGATOR	R5
OBSERVE	OBSERVATION	U15
ORGANISE	ORGANISER/ORGANISATION	U15
PARTICIPATE	PARTICIPANT/PARTICIPATION	U15
PLEASE	PLEASURE	U7
PRONOUNCE	PRONUNCIATION	U22
PUBLISH	PUBLISHER	U16
RADIATE	RADIATOR	R3
RELATE	RELATIVE	U1
SAIL	SAILING	U8
SPECTATE	SPECTATORS/SPECTACLE	U15
START	STARTER	U3
SUPPORT	SUPPORTER	U15
SYMPATHISE	SYMPATHY	U7
WEIGH	WEIGHT	U3

Close-Up B1 English in Use
Teacher's Book
Philip James

Publisher: Gavin McLean
Director of Content Development: Sarah Bideleux
Editorial Assistant: Sarah-Jane Platt
Project Editor: Amy Borthwick
Production Controller: Elaine Willis
Art Director: Natasa Arsenidou
Cover Designer: Tania Diakaki
Compositor: Sofia Fourtouni

Acknowledgements
Editorial and project management by hyphen SA

© 2013 National Geographic Learning, as part of Cengage Learning

ALL RIGHTS RESERVED. No part of this work covered by the copyright herein may be reproduced, transmitted, stored, or used in any form or by any means graphic, electronic, or mechanical, including but not limited to photocopying, recording, scanning, digitizing, taping, Web distribution, information networks, or information storage and retrieval systems, except as permitted under Section 107 or 108 of the 1976 United States Copyright Act, without the prior written permission of the publisher.

> For permission to use material from this text or product, submit all requests online at **www.cengage.com/permissions**
>
> Further permissions questions can be emailed to
> **permissionrequest@cengage.com**

ISBN: 978-1-4080-6167-1

National Geographic Learning
Cheriton House, North Way, Andover, Hampshire, SP10 5BE
United Kingdom

Cengage Learning is a leading provider of customized learning solutions with office locations around the globe, including Singapore, the United Kingdom, Australia, Mexico, Brazil and Japan. Locate your local office at: **international.cengage.com/region**

Cengage Learning products are represented in Canada by Nelson Education, Ltd.

Visit National Geographic Learning online at **ngl.cengage.com**

Visit our corporate website at **www.cengage.com**

Photo credits
Cover image: Shutterstock
All other images: Shutterstock

Lightning Source UK Ltd.
Milton Keynes UK
UKHW050008260621
386160UK00004B/29